KB197658

Korean for Travel Service

서비스 한국어

김은영 Kim Eun Young / 김공환 Kim Kong Hwan

박영사

머리말

    최근 전 세계적으로 한국어와 한국 문화에 대한 관심이 커져 가고 있으며, 한국 유학이나 한국 기업 취업에 대한 관심뿐 아니라 세계 각지에서 한국어와 한국 문화를 배우기 위한 열의가 높아지고 있다.

    이에 따라 이 책은 한국어 학습자의 다양한 성격과 수요를 반영하여 해외에서 한국인 관광객을 맞이하는 현지인들을 위해 고안된 비즈니스 여행 한국어 교재이다. 해외여행 관광산업 종사자들이 한국인 관광객과 함께 사용할 수 있는 여행 주제와 표현에 초점을 맞추고 있다. 또한 해외 여행 및 관광 산업의 수요를 충족시키기 위해 실제 상황에서 맥락에 따라 사용되는 단어, 대화, 응용 표현을 소개하였다.

    이 책의 내용은 현지인들이 한국인 관광객들과 소통할 수 있도록 공항 출입, 교통, 쇼핑, 관광 등 여행 상황 및 기능별 의사소통을 중심으로 내용을 구성하였다. 현지 가이드의 비즈니스 상황을 고려하여 격식체와 비격식체를 9개 단원에서 함께 다루며, 현지 가이드를 위한 초·중급 수준의 공식 대응 유형을 포함하고 있다. 또한 실제 상황에서 한국인들이 사용하는 문화적, 일상적 표현을 다양한 관용구와 함께 제시하였다.

    한국인 관광객을 안내하는 현지 가이드가 한국어로 쉽게 의사소통을 할 수 있도록 여행 어휘 사전을 수록하였으며, 여행 중 필수적인 응답 연습과 다양한 문장 패턴을 담고 있다. 또한, 교재에 있는 대화나 내용을 듣고 말하는 연습을 할 수 있도록 QR코드 형태의 음성 파일도 제공한다. 〈서비스 한국어〉를 통해 한국인 관광객을 안내하는 현지 가이드가 더 흥미롭고 효율적으로 한국어와 한국문화를 학습할 수 있기를 기대해 본다.

2025년 2월

저자

Preface

This book is a business travel Korean textbook designed for the locals welcoming Korean tourists overseas. It focuses on topics and expressions that overseas travel and tourism industry practitioners can use with Korean tourists. It introduces words, application expressions, and dialogues used contextually to meet the demand of the travel and tourism industry overseas.

To help the locals communicate with Korean tourists, the contents of this book are organized based on contextual and functional communication such as entry and exit at the airport, transportation, shopping, and tourism. It is composed of nine units which cover formal and informal expressions in consideration of business conditions and includes beginner and formal response types for the local guides. It utilizes cultural and everyday expressions used by Koreans in real-world situations and presents them together with various idiomatic phrases.

It contains a travel vocabulary dictionary and provides response practice and sentence patterns that are essential during travel, as well as voice files in QR forms that would allow the travel and tourism industry practitioners to practice listening and speaking, making it easier for them to communicate in Korean.

목차

Unit 1   **한글**

Hangeul, The Korean Alphabet 001

Unit 2   **저는 여행가이드예요**

I'm a tour guide 039

Unit 3   **실례지만 여권 좀 보여 주세요**

Excuse me, but please show me your passport............................. 067

Unit 4   **지금 주문하시겠습니까?**

May I take your order now?... 099

Unit 5   **편의점은 약국 옆에 있습니다**

The convenience store is next to the pharmacy 127

Unit 6   **오늘밤 공연 좌석은 매진됐습니다**

The seats for tonight's show are sold out....................................155

Unit 7   **스노클링을 해 본 적이 있으세요?**

Have you ever snorkeled?...183

Unit 8   **천천히 보시고 필요한 게 있으면 말씀해 주세요**

Take your time and let me know if you need anything.......................... 217

Unit 9   **곧 다른 버스를 대절하도록 하겠습니다**

We'll rent another bus soon... 245

Unit 10   **물병은 가방에 넣고 탑승하지 마세요**

Don't put a bottle of water in your bag before boarding 275

Appendix   **한국어 인사표현**

Korean greeting expression... 303

교재 단원 및 내용 구성(Tourism Korean Table of Contents)

Ch.	Title	Topic	Dialogue
1	한글	한글 알파벳 Hangeul Alphabet	
2	저는 여행가이드예요	인사와 소개 Greeting and Introduction	1. 소개와 인사 2. 환영 인사와 안내 3. 일행 소개
3	실례지만 여권 좀 보여 주세요	숙박과 호텔 Accommodation and Hotel	1. 체크인 2. 체크아웃 3. 호텔 서비스 요청
4	지금 주문하시겠습니까?	식당과 음식 Ordering Foods and Restaurant	1. 주문받기 1 – 레스토랑 2. 주문받기 2 – 패스트푸드점 3. 주문받기 3 – 룸서비스
5	편의점은 약국 옆에 있습니다	위치와 방향, 교통수단 Location and Direction, Transportation	1. 위치와 방향 2. 길 찾기 3. 렌터카 대여
6	오늘밤 공연 좌석은 매진됐습니다	관람과 체험, 방문과 견학 Excursion and Field trips	1. 공연 예약 2. 박물관 견학 3. 시설 방문
7	스노클링을 해 본 적이 있으세요?	여행과 관광 Travel and Sightseeing	1. 관광 상품 안내 2. 여행지 추천 3. 사진 촬영
8	천천히 보시고 필요한 게 있으면 말씀해 주세요	쇼핑 안내와 판매 Shopping guide and Sales	1. 방문 고객 응대 2. 제품 안내와 흥정 3. 환불 및 계산
9	곧 다른 버스를 대절하 도록 하겠습니다	응급상황과 질병 Travel troubles and Emergency	1. 사고 2. 도난과 분실 3. 부상과 질병
10	물병은 가방에 넣고 탑승하지 마세요	도움과 요청 Offering help and Giving advice	1. 출국장 2. 은행 3. 우체국
Appendix	한국어 인사표현		

Grammar	Culture Tips	pronunciation
– 은/는, –이에요/예요, –아/어/여요 – ㅂ습니다/습니까?, –입니다/입니까?, –(으)시 – 에서, –도, 무슨, –이/가 아니다	– 한국의 언어 문화 – 한국인의 인사법과 호칭	받침규칙
– (으)ㄹ까요?, –고 싶다, –아/어/여 주세요, 　– 지만 – 이/가, –(으)로[1], –겠 – 시간과 날짜, 안–하다, –지 않다	– 한국의 기념일 – 한국의 전통 명절	경음화
– 단위명사, –주세요, –하고 – (으)ㄹ 거예요, (이)나, –은/는 어떠세요? – 을/를, –(으)ㄴ데요, –만	– 전형적인 한식탁 – 한국인의 식사예절	비음화
– 에, –아/어/여서[1], (순서), –(으)로[2] – 에서 –까지, –이/가 걸리다, 못–하다 – 동안, –(으)ㄴ데, –았/었/였	– 한국의 교통관련 문화 – 한국인의 가족 관계와 호칭	격음화
– (으)ㄴ/는, –나요?, –아/어/여 있다 – 아/어/여도 되다, –(으)면 안 되다, –마다 – 기 전에, –아/어/여야 하다(되다)	– 한국인의 감정 표현 신조어 – 한국의 사계절과 계절활동&축제 – 한국인이 좋아하는 취미	연음
– (으)ㄴ 적이 있다/없다, –아/어/여보다, –(으)ㄹ 수 있다/없다 – (으)ㄹ 만하다, 가장–하다, –고[1] – (으)ㄴ 후에, –에 대해(서)	– 한국인이 해외여행을 많이 가는 시기 – 한국인의 요즘 해외여행 추세 – 한국 관광객들의 특징과 습관	유음화
– 고[2], –(으)면 – 고 있다, –(으)ㄴ 것 같다, –네요 – 에 비해(서), –보다, –아/어/여 보이다	– 세계 주요 국가의 화폐단위 – 한국의 화폐 – 한국인들이 관심 갖는 쇼핑 품목	구개음화
– 도록, –(으)ㄹ 뻔하다 – 아/어/여 버리다, –(으)ㄹ 때, –아/어/여서[2] (이유) – (으)ㄴ 지, –고 나서, –아/어/여지다	– 한국의 의료&의약 서비스 체계 – 건강한 삶을 위한 일상 수칙 10가지 – 한국 사람들의 인터넷 활용	'ㅎ' 약화
– 지요, –덕분에, –지 마세요 – 고 말고요, –는 대로 – 지 않다, –(으)려고 하다, –때문에	– 한국의 국적 항공사와 저비용 항공사 – 한국의 국제공항	'의' 발음

1

한글
Hangeul, The Korean Alphabet

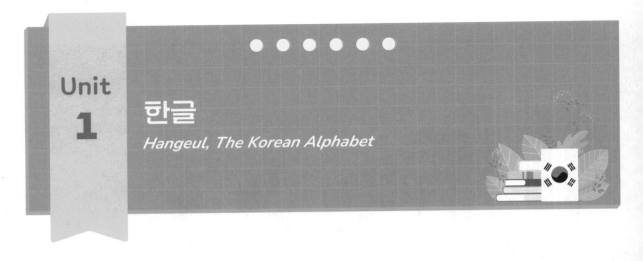

Unit 1

한글

Hangeul, The Korean Alphabet

Introduction to Hangeul

Hangeul is the name of the unique Korean alphabet created in 1446 by King Sejong the Great and scholars of the time. Since King Sejong's goal was to increase literacy in the country, he wanted to make Hangeul as easy as possible for the people.

Just like the English alphabet, Hangeul contains consonants and vowels. The five basic consonants (ㄱ, ㄴ, ㅁ, ㅅ, ㅇ) follow the shape of the speech organs as they make the sound while the remainder were made by adding strokes to the basic consonants. The vowels are a combination of the symbols '•', '—', and 'ㅣ' which represent the sun in the sky, the flat earth, and standing human beings, respectively. All vowels are composed of these three elements.

Modern Hangeul consists of 19 consonants and 21 vowels. There are certain rules for constructing the letters within a syllable in Korean:

1. Each syllable begins with a consonant. When the syllable technically only consists of a vowel, it gets combined together with the letter ㅇ, so the first letter is still a consonant. For example, the Korean vowel ㅗ is not written ㅗ but as 오.
2. The way each syllable is constructed depends on the vowel used. If it's a vertical vowel, in other words, ㅣ, ㅏ, ㅓ, and so on, then the initial consonant is placed on the left side of the vowel.

$$\square + \vdash = 마$$

If the vowel is horizontal, so ㅜ, ㅡ, ㅗ, and so on, then the first consonant should be placed above the vowel.

$$\square + \bot = 모$$

3. It is possible to have one final consonant, two final consonants, or none.

4. If a syllable shows a consonant–vowel–consonant combination, in other words, if a syllable ends with a consonant, called "batchim", the final consonant goes to the bottom of that syllable.

$$ㄴ + \vdash + \square = 남$$
$$ㄴ + \bot + \square = 놈$$

5. Each syllable is written in a square box.

All symbols of Hangeul are written from top to bottom and from left to right. Strokes are never interrupted, not even when they change directions halfway.

Korean has four basic syllable structures: 'V', "VC', "CV', and 'CVC'.

안	녕	하	세	요	한	글
						C
V	C V				C V	V
		C V	C V	V		
C	C				C	C

1 Vowels

The positive, or "Yang" vowels were created by adding • to the right side of ㅣ and to the top of ㅡ, resulting in ㅏ and ㅗ, while the negative, or "Yin" vowels were created by adding • to the left side of ㅣ and the bottom of ㅡ, resulting in ㅓ and ㅜ. Next, one extra stroke was added to each of these to form the two positive vowels ㅑ, and ㅛ, and the two negative vowels ㅕ and ㅠ.

Korean has 10 basic vowels (ㅏ, ㅑ, ㅓ, ㅕ, ㅗ, ㅛ, ㅜ, ㅠ, ㅡ, ㅣ) and 11 compound vowels (ㅐ, ㅒ, ㅔ, ㅖ, ㅘ, ㅙ, ㅚ, ㅝ, ㅞ, ㅟ, ㅢ).

1.1 Basic Vowels

Track 1-01

Vowel	Pronunciation	Stroke Order
ㅏ	as in "car"	
ㅑ	as in "yawn"	
ㅓ	as in "up"	
ㅕ	as in "yearn"	
ㅗ	as in "old"	
ㅛ	as in "yo!"	
ㅜ	as in "glue"	

ㅠ	as in "y<u>oo</u>"	① → ②↓ ㅜ ㅠ↓③
ㅡ	as in "sev<u>e</u>n"	① →
ㅣ	as in "tr<u>ee</u>"	ㅣ①↓

Listen to the following

Track 1-02

아　　야　　어　　여　　오　　요　　우　　유　　으　　이

The soundless "ㅇ"

In spoken Korean, a vowel can be pronounced as an independent syllable. In writing, however, a vowel cannot stand alone. Either a consonant or a soundless 'ㅇ' must be written in front of the vowel for balance. The consonant 'ㅇ' can be used at the beginning of the syllable to give an empty sound. Remember that in order to make a sound or a syllable in Korean we need at least one consonant and one vowel together.

Listen to the audio and check the syllables you hear

Track 1-03

1) ⓐ 으 ☐　　　　ⓑ 우 ☐
2) ⓐ 이 ☐　　　　ⓑ 으 ☐
3) ⓐ 오 ☐　　　　ⓑ 아 ☐
4) ⓐ 어 ☐　　　　ⓑ 오 ☐

Read the following words

Track 1-04

우유　　　　　여우　　　　　아이　　　　　오이

Write the basic vowels while reading it

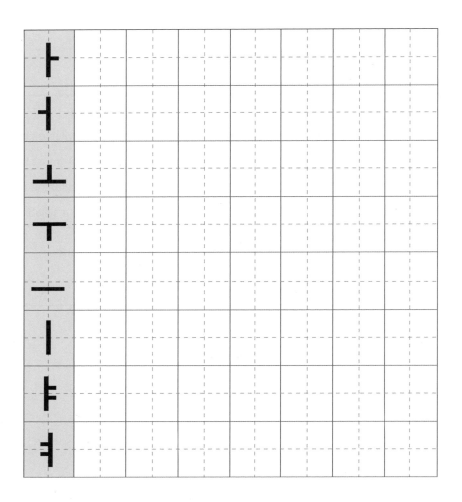

Write the following words

Listen to the audio and complete the following words Track 1-05

1) 아
2) 유
3) 이
4) 오

1.2 Compound Vowels

Vowel	Pronunciation	Stroke Order
ㅐ	as in "b<u>a</u>t"	
ㅒ	as in "<u>yeh</u>"	
ㅔ	as in "<u>e</u>gg"	
ㅖ	as in "<u>yeh</u>"	
ㅘ	as in "<u>w</u>ant"	
ㅙ	as in "<u>whe</u>n"	
ㅚ	as in "<u>wa</u>y"	
ㅝ	as in "<u>wa</u>r"	
ㅞ	as in "<u>we</u>nt"	
ㅟ	as in "<u>wee</u>d"	
ㅢ	as in "b<u>ooey</u>"	

Write the following vowels

ㅐ							
ㅕ							
ㅗ							
ㅜ							
ㅛ							
ㅠ							
ㅘ							
ㅝ							
ㅙ							
ㅞ							
ㅣ							

Phonetically speaking, Korean vowels are divided into 10 monophthongs (short vowels) (ㅏ, ㅓ, ㅗ, ㅜ, ㅡ, ㅣ, ㅐ, ㅔ, ㅚ, ㅟ) and 11 diphthongs (vowel combinations) (ㅑ, ㅕ, ㅛ, ㅠ, ㅒ, ㅖ, ㅘ, ㅙ, ㅝ, ㅞ, ㅢ). When pronouncing a single monophthong, the shape of the lips and position of the tongue do not change; monophthongs can thus be differentiated by the degree to which the mouth opens and the position of the tongue. However, in the case of diphthongs, the shape of the lips and position of the tongue change as the vowel is pronounced. Note, however, that ㅚ and ㅟ are often pronounced as the diphthongs [oe] and [wi], respectively.

Diphthongs			
ㅑ	ㅣ + ㅏ	ㅘ	ㅗ + ㅏ
ㅕ	ㅣ + ㅓ	ㅙ	ㅗ + ㅐ
ㅛ	ㅣ + ㅗ	ㅝ	ㅜ + ㅓ
ㅠ	ㅣ + ㅜ	ㅞ	ㅜ + ㅔ
ㅒ	ㅣ + ㅐ	ㅢ	ㅡ + ㅣ
ㅖ	ㅣ + ㅖ		

Listen to the following

외　워　웨　위　의　애　얘　에　예　와　왜

Pronunciation Tips

1. 'ㅔ' and 'ㅐ' are supposed to be distinguishable in pronunciation, but in many cases they are not distinguishable these days. (에 = 애)

2. 'ㅚ', 'ㅙ' and 'ㅞ' also tend to be pronounced the same as [wɛ] or [we].

3. 'ㅖ' is pronounced as [ㅖ] in '예' and "례", but in all other cases it can be pronounced as [ㅔ]

4. The six compound vowels [w] are pronounced by starting with the lips rounded and pronouncing ㅗ or ㅜ and then adding a basic vowel sound.

$$ㅗ + ㅏ = ㅘ$$
$$ㅗ + ㅐ = ㅙ$$
$$ㅗ + ㅣ = ㅚ$$
$$ㅜ + ㅓ = ㅝ$$
$$ㅜ + ㅔ = ㅞ$$
$$ㅜ + ㅣ = ㅟ$$

5. The vowel ㅢ is pronounced by pronouncing ㅡ and ㅣ as quickly as possible and as a single syllable.

$$ㅡ + ㅣ = ㅢ$$

2 Consonants

Five basic consonant letters (ㄱ, ㄴ, ㅁ, ㅅ, ㅇ) were created based on the shape of the articulatory organs involved in their production. 'ㄱ' represents the root of the tongue blocking the oral cavity, 'ㄴ', the tongue touching the front of the roof of the mouth, 'ㅁ', the shape of the opened lips, 'ㅅ', the shape of the mouth when blowing air between the teeth, and 'ㅇ', the oral cavity opened wide. Further, with the addition of one or two strokes to these basic consonants, the additional consonants 'ㅋ, ㄷ, ㅌ, ㅂ, ㅍ, ㅈ, ㅊ', and 'ㅎ' were created, while the compound consonants 'ㄲ, ㄸ, ㅃ, ㅆ', and 'ㅉ' were created by combining two consonants side by side. With the inclusion of the additional consonant 'ㄹ', there are a total of 19 consonants used in modern Korean.

Plain Consonants		Aspirated Consonants	Tense Consonants
Basic			
ㄱ		ㅋ	ㄲ
ㄴ	ㄷ, ㄹ	ㅌ	ㄸ
ㅁ	ㅂ	ㅍ	ㅃ
ㅅ	ㅈ	ㅊ	ㅆ, ㅉ
ㅇ			

Basic Consonant

Vowel	Pronunciation	Stroke Order
ㄱ	[k] as in "pea<u>k</u>" [g] as in "<u>g</u>arden"	ㄱ
ㄴ	[n] as in "noo<u>n</u>"	ㄴ
ㄷ	[t] as in "ea<u>t</u>" [d] as in "<u>d</u>ear"	ㄷ
ㄹ	[r] as in "<u>r</u>abbit" [l] as in "foo<u>l</u>"	ㄹ
ㅁ	[m] as in "<u>m</u>any"	ㅁ
ㅂ	[p] as in "to<u>p</u>" [b] as in "<u>b</u>ank"	ㅂ
ㅅ	[s] as in "<u>s</u>on" [ʃ] as in "<u>sh</u>ed"	ㅅ
ㅇ	[ng] as in "lo<u>ng</u>"	ㅇ
ㅈ	[j] as in "<u>j</u>oy"	ㅈ
ㅊ	[ch] as in "<u>ch</u>ange"	ㅊ
ㅋ	[k] as in "<u>k</u>ing"	ㅋ
ㅌ	[t] as in "<u>t</u>ime"	ㅌ
ㅍ	[p] as in "<u>p</u>en"	ㅍ
ㅎ	[h] as in "<u>h</u>igh"	ㅎ

Write the basic consonants while reading each of them

ㄱ							
ㄴ							
ㄷ							
ㄹ							
ㅁ							
ㅂ							
ㅅ							
ㅇ							
ㅈ							
ㅊ							
ㅋ							
ㅌ							
ㅍ							
ㅎ							

Read the following along with what you hear

	ㅏ	ㅑ	ㅓ	ㅕ	ㅗ	ㅛ	ㅜ	ㅠ	ㅡ	ㅣ
ㄱ	가	갸	거	겨	고	교	구	규	그	기
ㄴ	나	냐	너	녀	노	뇨	누	뉴	느	니
ㄷ	다	댜	더	뎌	도	됴	두	듀	드	디
ㄹ	라	랴	러	려	로	료	루	류	르	리
ㅁ	마	먀	머	며	모	묘	무	뮤	므	미
ㅂ	바	뱌	버	벼	보	뵤	부	뷰	브	비
ㅅ	사	샤	서	셔	소	쇼	수	슈	스	시
ㅇ	아	야	어	여	오	요	우	유	으	이
ㅈ	자	쟈	저	져	조	죠	주	쥬	즈	지
ㅊ	차	챠	처	쳐	초	쵸	추	츄	츠	치
ㅋ	카	캬	커	켜	코	쿄	쿠	큐	크	키
ㅌ	타	탸	터	텨	토	툐	투	튜	트	티
ㅍ	파	퍄	퍼	펴	포	표	푸	퓨	프	피
ㅎ	하	햐	허	혀	호	효	후	휴	흐	히

Read the following words

Track 1-09

나무

다리

어머니

비누

기차 타조 피아노 휴지

Complete the following table

	ㅏ	ㅑ	ㅓ	ㅕ	ㅗ	ㅛ	ㅜ	ㅠ	ㅡ	ㅣ
ㄱ	가									
ㄴ		냐								
ㄷ			더							
ㄹ				려						
ㅁ					모					
ㅂ						뵤				
ㅅ							수			
ㅇ								유		
ㅈ									즈	
ㅊ										치
ㅋ	카									
ㅌ		탸								
ㅍ			퍼							
ㅎ				혀						

Write the following words

가수

아기

가구

나무

호수

바지

구두

바나나

라디오

Read the following words

Track 1-10

개미 (Ant)	노래 (Song)	새 (Bird)	세로 (Vertical)	게 (Crab)
베개 (Pillow)	얘기 (Story)	쟤 (He/She)	세계 (World)	예쁘다 (Pretty)
예의 (Etiquette)	과자 (Snacks)	사과 (Apple)	와이파이 (Wi-Fi)	돼지 (Pig)
왜 (Why)	뇌 (Brain)	외우다 (Memorize)	회사 (Company)	뭐 (What)
샤워 (Shower)	더워요 (Hot)	스웨터 (Sweater)	웨이터 (Waiter)	가위 (Scissors)
뛰다 (Run)	위 (Stomach)	의자 (Chair)	의사 (Doctor)	회의 (Meeting)

Write the following words

예 의					
과 자					
사 과					
회 사					
샤 워					
가 위					
뛰 다					

예쁘다											
외우다											
더워요											
스웨터											
웨이터											
추워요											

새									
게									
뭐									
위									
뇌									
쟤									
왜									

2.2 Double Consonants

Track 1-11

Double Consonants	ㄲ	ㄸ	ㅃ	ㅆ	ㅉ
Stroke Order	ㄲ	ㄸ	ㅃ	ㅆ	ㅉ

Korean consonants can be classified as neutral, aspirated, and tense depending on syllable formation. This system is a unique feature of Korean. The neutral form has no strong release of air or tension, while aspirated consonants are accompanied by a strong release of air. Tense consonants are called so because they are pronounced with the tongue muscles tensed.

Neutral	Aspirated	Tense
ㄱ	ㅋ	ㄲ
ㄷ	ㅌ	ㄸ
ㅂ	ㅍ	ㅃ
ㅅ		ㅆ
ㅈ	ㅊ	ㅉ

Write the following double consonants

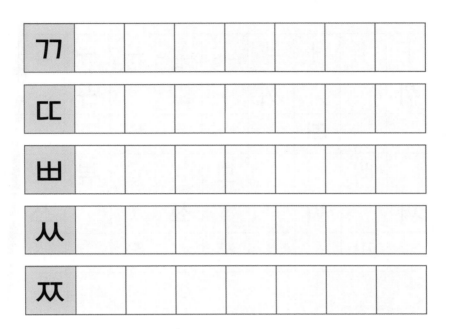

ㄲ						

ㄸ						

ㅃ						

ㅆ						

ㅉ						

Listen to the following

Track 1-12

가 까 카 다 따 타 바 빠 파 사 싸 자 짜 차

Write the syllables by combining double consonants with basic vowels.

	ㅏ	ㅑ	ㅓ	ㅕ	ㅗ	ㅛ	ㅜ	ㅠ	ㅡ	ㅣ
ㄲ	까			껴	꼬		꾸			
ㄸ			떠				뚜			뜨
ㅃ		빠			뽀			뷰		삐
ㅆ	싸		써			쑈		쓰		
ㅉ		쨔			쪼		쭈			찌

Read the following words

Track 1-13

비싸다 (expensive)	짜다 (salty)	뽀뽀 (kiss)	쓰레기 (trash)	까치 (magpie)
허리띠 (belt)	씨 (seed)	뻐꾸기 (cuckoo)	쓰다 (write)	아빠 (dad)
뿌리 (root)	끄다 (turn-off)	꼬리 (tail)	뜨다 (float)	찌개 (stew)

Read and write the following words

Track 1-14

싸다					
꼬리					
토끼					
아빠					
뽀뽀					
뿌리					

쓰다					
짜다					
까치					
타조					
포도					
기차					

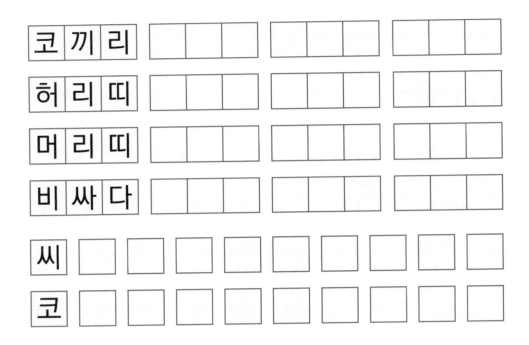

코	끼	리									
허	리	띠									
머	리	띠									
비	싸	다									
씨									
코									

Listen carefully, and choose the correct syllable

Track 1-15

1) ① 짜　　② 싸

2) ① 짜　　② 빠

3) ① 타　　② 파

4) ① 차　　② 카

5) ① 까　　② 따

3　Syllables

When the basic vowels introduced earlier are used by themselves with no consonants, they are combined with the consonant 'ㅇ' to form complete syllables. In this case the initial 'ㅇ' is not voiced, but silent. Korean has the following syllable structures.

3.1　Vowel (V)

(V) syllables consist of a single vowel. There are two main types, those formed from the vertical vowels such as '아', '어' or '이' and those formed from the horizontal vowels including '오', '우', or '으'. The stroke order for syllables follows the same two principles used when writing the consonants and vowels: "left to right" and "top to bottom."

ㅇ + ㅓ = 어　　　　ㅇ + ㅗ = 오

3.2　Consonant (C) + Vowel (V)

(C) + (V) syllables consist of one consonant and one vowel. There are two types, those that combine horizontally and those that combine vertically. The vertical syllable '다', for example, is written with 'ㄷ' beside 'ㅏ' instead of below it (ㄷ/ㅏ). In this way, consonants and vowels are combined to form single-character syllables. The syllable '고' is written according to the sample principle, that is, writing 'ㄱ' above 'ㅗ' to form a single character instead of writing them separately as ㄱㅗ.

ㄷ + ㅏ = 다　　　　ㄱ + ㅗ = 고

3.3　Consonant (C) + Vowel (V) + Consonant (C)

(C)+(V)+(C) syllables consist of a consonant, and vowel followed by a final consonant (called batchim, 받침).

ㅂ + ㅏ + ㅇ = 방　　　　ㅅ + ㅗ + ㄴ = 손

3.4　Consonant (C) + Vowel (V) + Double Consonant (CC)

(C)+(V)+(CC) syllables include a consonant and vowel followed by a final consonant consisting of a double consonant.

$$ㄱ + ㅏ + ㅄ = 값 \qquad ㅎ + ㅡ + ㄺ = 흙$$
$$ㄷ + ㅏ + ㄺ = 닭 \qquad ㅅ + ㅏ + ㄻ = 삶$$

4 Final Consonants

The final consonant in the *Hangeul* syllable is called a *batchim*. Final consonants that form the end of syllables are pronounced somewhat differently than initial consonants. While initial consonants are pronounced fully according to their original phonetic value along with the vowels that follow them, final consonants are reduced to the representative sound of their respective organ of articulation.

While all of the *Hangeul* consonants can be used as final consonants, they can only be expressed as 7 sounds: ㄱ, ㄴ, ㄷ, ㄹ, ㅁ, ㅂ, and ㅇ. For example, both ㄱ and ㅋ as final consonants are pronounced [k] ㄷ, ㅅ, ㅈ, ㅊ, ㅌ, and ㅎ as final consonants are pronounced [t] and ㅂ and ㅍ as final consonants are pronounced [p]. As for ㅇ, when it is used as a final consonant, it is pronounced [ng].

$$ㅎ + ㅏ + ㄴ = 한$$

$$ㄱ + ㅜ + ㄱ = 국$$

Final Consonant	Sound	Examples
ㄱ, ㅋ	[k]	억, 엌
ㄴ	[n]	온
ㄷ, ㅅ, ㅈ, ㅊ, ㅌ, ㅎ	[t]	옫, 옷, 옺, 옻, 옽, 옿
ㄹ	[l]	알

ㅁ	[m]	암
ㅂ, ㅍ	[p]	압, 앞
ㅇ	[ng]	앙

Read the following words

Track 1-16

Sound	Example words	
[k]	수박 watermelon	밖 outside
	부엌 kitchen	닭 chicken

Sound	Example words	
[n]	산 mountain	시간 time
	돈 money	사진 photo

Sound	Example words	
[t]	듣다 hear	옷 clothes
	낮 daytime	꽃 flower
	밑 under	놓다 put

Sound	Example words	
[l]	발 foot	겨울 winter
	쌀 rice	과일 fruit

[m]	김치 kimchi	이름 name
	봄 spring	감기 cold

[p]	집 house	지갑 wallet
	잎 leaf	무릎 knee

[ng]	가방 bag	시장 market
	화장실 rest room	병원 hospital

Compound final consonants refer to syllables in which there are two final consonants. In the case of compound consonants, there are two possible rules of pronunciation: either the first consonant is pronounced as the representative sound, or the second consonant is pronounced. For example, syllables ending in ㄳ, ㄶ, ㄵ, ㄼ, ㄾ and ㅄ only the first consonant is voiced, while in syllables ending in ㄺ, ㄻ, ㄿ only the second consonant is voiced.

① **When pronouncing the first consonant in double final consonant:**

삯[삭]   많다[만타]   앉다[안따]   Track 1-17

여덟[여덜]   핥다[할따]   값[갑]

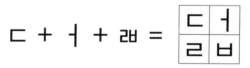

② **When pronouncing the second consonant in double final consonant:**

닭[닥]   삶[삼]   읊다[읍따]

Track 1-18

$$ ㅅ + ㅏ + ㄹㅁ = \boxed{\begin{array}{cc} ㅅ & ㅏ \\ ㄹ & ㅁ \end{array}} $$

Pronunciation Point

The final consonants ㅂ and ㅍ, ㄱ, ㅋ, and ㄲ, ㄷ, ㅌ, ㅅ, ㅈ, ㅊ, ㅎ and ㅆ, have the same sound but different meanings.

Track 1-19

입 mouth   박 gourd   빗 comb

잎 leaf   밖 outside   빚 debt

                                    빛 light

Final Consonant	Sound	Examples
ㄲ	[k]	깎다
ㅆ	[t]	있다
ㄵ, ㄶ	[n]	앉다, 많다
ㄽ, ㄾ, ㅀ, ㄼ, ㄻ	[l]	핥다, 끓다, 넓다
ㅄ	[p]	값
ㄺ	[k]	읽다
ㄻ	[m]	삶다

Complete the following tables by adding batchim and read letters

	ㄱ	ㄴ	ㄷ	ㄹ	ㅁ	ㅂ	ㅇ
가	각						
나		난					
다			닫				
라				랄			
마					맘		
바						밥	
아							앙

Read and write the following words

Track 1-20

같다					
낚시					
알다					
앉다					
무릎					
걷다					
시간					
수박					
가방					
이름					
과일					
얼굴					

| 숟 | 가 | 락 | | | | | | | | | |

숟	가	락									
하	얗	다									
잎	사	귀									
찜	질	방									
편	의	점									

책									
눈									
밤									
입									
집									
빗									

방									
낮									
옆									
빛									
꽃									
닭									

Listen carefully, and choose the correct syllable

Track 1-21

1) ① 돗 　　　② 돔
2) ① 갈 　　　② 갓
3) ① 잡 　　　② 잔
4) ① 솔 　　　② 솟
5) ① 막 　　　② 맡

5　Sentences

Basic Korean sentence structure is made up of a subject, object, and verb structure. Looking at this sentence structure, we can say that it is quite different from how English sentences are structured. Another thing that differentiates it from another foreign language, like the English language, is the usage of subject and object markers.

The basic Korean sentence structure is Subject, Object, Verb (SOV).

저는 새를 봐요.　(Subject – Object – Verb)

'저는 새를 봐요' would literally translate to "I the bird see." This sentence follows the subject–object–verb pattern. It's important to know that verbs (and adjectives) almost always come at the end of a sentence.

5.1 Subject – Verb

The subject verb pattern is one of the most common of the basic Korean sentence structures.

나는 먹고 싶어요　(Subject – Verb)

This sentence means "I want to eat" in English.

5.2 Subject – Adjective

This Korean sentence structure is like the one above, except you're going to swap out the verb with an adjective.

나는 행복해요.　(Subject – Adjective)

This Korean sentence means "I am happy" in English.

5.3 Subject – Object – Verb

The next Korean sentence structure is just like the first one, except there is already an object added to the sentence.

나는 불고기를 먹어요.　(Subject – Object – Verb)

In this Korean sentence, the object refers to the noun "불고기".

5.4 Subject of a Korean Sentence

Using the subject in a Korean sentence is optional.

"나는 불고기를 먹어요" can also be written as "불고기를 먹어요."

In this case, the subject ("I") is understood. Therefore, you can drop it from the sentence. Koreans often do this to simplify their speech.

5.5 Korean Particles (Markers)

In addition to Korean grammar and conjugations, you should also be aware of Korean markers, or particles, when learning Korean. We don't use them in English, so they may be a new grammar concept to you.

Once you get the hang of basic sentence structures, then you can start to add Korean particles into your conversations. Keep in mind that Koreans often omit the Korean particles from sentences in spoken Korean. However, they're important pieces of Korean grammar that you will likely see in written form.

Topic vs. Subject Marker:

Both topic marker (은/는) and subject marker (이/가) are used for the sentence's subject. '은/는' serves as a theme, contrast, or emphasis whereas '이/가' is used to provide new topics or information while acting as a subject marker. The difference is the emphasis that the particle places on the sentence. The topic marker puts the emphasis on the verb, while the subject marker places emphasis on the subject.

나는 새를 봤어요.   I **saw** a bird. (는: topic marker)

내가 새를 봤어요.   It's **me** who saw a bird. (가: subject marker)

Object Marker:

The markers (particles) '를' and '을' are used to indicate the object of a sentence. The object in a sentence in Korean is similar to the object in a sentence in English.

나는 피자를 먹었어요.   I ate pizza. (Subject-Object-Verb)

The object, in this case, is '피자.'

There are more particles such as place marker used in Korean sentence structure.

Answers

Track 1- 03	(1) 우	(2) 으	(3) 오	(4) 어	
Track 1- 05	(1) 우	(2) 이	(3) 아	(4) 이	
Track 1- 15	(1) 싸	(2) 짜	(3) 타	(4) 카	(5) 따
Track 1- 21	(1) 돔	(2) 갓	(3) 잡	(4) 솔	(5) 맡

메모

2

저는 여행가이드예요
I'm a tour guide

Unit 2

저는 여행가이드예요
I'm a tour guide

---

1 **Study Objectives** 학습 목표

🖊 To know Korean greeting/introduction expressions. (인사와 소개)

🖊 To greet tourists in Korean at the airport (공항 도착 인사)

🖊 To guide the guests to their accommodation using Korean (숙소 안내)

🖊 To learn general customer service in Korean (고객 서비스)

---

2 **Vocabulary** 어휘

2.1 **Dialogue Vocabulary** 본문 어휘

Noun 명사 🖊

저 I (honorific)	여행 travel/tour	가이드 guide	이름 name
베트남 Vietnam	여행사 travel agency	다낭 Danang	호텔 hotel
한국 Korea	중국 China	사람 person	중국 사람 Chinese
학생 student	선생님 teacher	한국어 Korean	영어 English
일 work	은행 bank	은행원 bank clerk	가족 family
부모님 parents (honorific)			

Verb 동사 ✏️

만나다 meet 　　실례하다 excuse 　　환영하다 welcome 　오다 come

감사하다 Thank you 　뵙다 see(honorific) 　모시다 serve

Others 나머지 ✏️

처음 first time 　　잘 well 　　　먼저 first 　　　반갑다 glad/pleasant

무슨 what kind of 　어디 where 　　제 my 　　　　씨 Mr., Miss, Mrs., Ms.

2.2 Related Vocabulary 관련 어휘

나라 Country ✏️

중국 China 　　　　　미국 United States 　　러시아 Russia

태국 Thailand 　　　라오스 Laos 　　　　캄보디아 Cambodia

미얀마 Myanmar 　　말레이시아 Malaysia 　필리핀 Philippines

싱가포르 Singapore 　인도네시아 Indonesia 　인도 India

네팔 Nepal 　　　　독일 Germany 　　　프랑스 France

스페인 Spain 　　　영국 United Kingdom 　캐나다 Canada

멕시코 Mexico 　　　브라질 Brazil 　　　호주 Australia

이집트 Egypt 　　　우간다 Uganda

직업 Occupation ✏️

의사 doctor 　　　　　　　요리사 chef 　　　　　기자 reporter

회사원 company employee 　연구원 researcher 　경찰 policeman

가수 singer 　　　　　　　간호사 nurse 　　　　변호사 lawyer

비서 secretary 　　　　　　군인 soldier 　　　　주부 housewife

사업가 entrepreneur 　　　미용사 hairdresser 　점원 store clerk

택시 기사 taxi driver 　　　운동 선수 athlete 　배우 actor

약사 pharmacist	소방관 fireman	모델 model
과학자 scientist	기술자 technician	교수 professor
회계사 accountant	우체부 postman	화가 artist / painter
여행(관광) 가이드 tour guide	패션 디자이너 fashion designer	

3 Dialogue 대화

Track 2-01

Dialogue 1 Introduction and Greetings 소개와 인사

A 안녕하세요? Hello.

B 네, 안녕하세요? Yeah, hello.

A 저는 여행 가이드예요. 제 이름은 꾸안이에요.
I'm a tour guide. My name is Quan.

B 안녕하세요. 저는 미선이에요. 만나서 반가워요.
Hello, I'm Misun. Nice to meet you.

–은/는

'은/는', topic marker, follows a noun, indicating that preceding noun is the topic of the sentence.

Nouns ending with a vowel → 는	Nouns ending with a consonant → 은
저 + 는 → 저는	이름 + 은 → 이름은

저는 여행 가이드예요. I'm a tour guide.	제 이름은 푸엉이에요. My name is Phoung.
민수 씨는 학생이에요. Minsoo is a student.	제 직업은 의사예요. My job is a doctor.
사과는 빨개요. Apples are red.	선생님은 한국 사람이에요. Teacher is a Korean.

🍀 **Circle the correct particle as shown in the example.**

Ex   제 이름(은 /(는))현수예요.

(1) 저(은 / 는) 학생이에요.

(2) 미쉘(은 / 는) 제 동생이에요.

(3) 존슨(은 / 는) 영국 사람이에요.

(4) 준영 씨(은 / 는) 한국 사람이에요.

–이에요/예요

'이에요/예요' attaches to a noun and is used to give statements or to ask a question in an informal situation.

Nouns ending with a vowel → –예요	Nouns ending with a consonant → –이에요
수미 + 예요 → 수미예요 의사 + 예요? → 의사예요?	예린 + 이에요 → 예린이에요 선생님 + 이에요? → 선생님이에요?

이름이 뭐예요? What is your name?
저는 박민수예요. I'm Park Minsoo.
안나는 미용사예요. Anna is a hairdresser.

메이는 태국 사람이에요. May is a Thai.
조셉은 학생이에요. Joseph is a student.
언니는 모델이에요. My older sister is a model.

♣ **Fill in the blanks by choosing the correct form between** '–이에요/예요' **as shown in the example.**

Ex 저는 정애리예요.

(1) 푸엉은 회사원_____.

(2) 제 이름은 토니_____.

(3) 다니엘 씨는 의사_____.

(4) 저는 필리핀 사람_____.

−아/어/여요

'−아/어/여요' is attached to the stem of a verb stem or an adjective stem and is used mostly in colloquial speech. Depending on your intonation, '−아/어/여요' is used for interrogatives, imperatives or suggestions.

'−아요' is attached to stems ending in the vowels ㅏ or ㅗ.	'−어요' is attached to stems ending in other vowels.	'−여요' is attached to stems ending in −하다.
가다: 가 + −아요 → 가아요 → 가요 (* An extra '아' isn't added.) 보다: 보 + −아요 → 보아요 → 봐요 좋다: 좋 + −아요 → 좋아요	먹다: 먹 + −어요 → 먹어요 있다: 있 + −어요 → 있어요 예쁘다: 예쁘 + −어요 → 예뻐요 (* 'ㅡ' dropped) 재미없다: 재미없 + −어요 → 재미없어요	공부하다: 공부하 + −여요 → 공부하여요 → 공부해요 (*−하 + −여요 is written in the contracted form of −해요.)

집에 가요? Are you going home?

돈 있어요? Do you have money?

민수 씨가 쇼핑해요. Minsoo shops.

마이클 씨가 한국어를 공부해요. Michael studies Korean.

이따 봐요. See you later.

그 여자는 예뻐요. That girl is pretty.

🍀 **Use the words in parentheses and fill in the blanks as shown in the example.**

> Ex 친구를 <u>만나요</u>. (만나다)

(1) 캐럴 씨가 공항에 _____. (가다)

(2) 이 식당이 _____ (넓다)

(3) 오늘 점심에 냉면을 _____. (먹다)

(4) 친구하고 _____. (전화하다)

A (실례합니다) 안녕하세요? 처음 뵙겠습니다.
(Excuse me.) Hello. It's a great pleasure to meet you.

저는 베트남 여행사 가이드 꾸안입니다.
I'm Guan, the guide of the Vietnamese travel agency

B 안녕하세요. 반갑습니다. Hello. Nice to meet you.

저는 김지혜입니다. I am Kim, Jihye.

A 환영합니다. 다낭에 잘 오셨습니다. Welcome. Welcome to Da Nang.

B 나와 주셔서 감사합니다. Thank you for coming to meet me.

A 그럼, 먼저 호텔로 모시겠습니다. Then, I'll take you to the hotel first.

B 네, 고맙습니다. Yes, Thank you.

-ㅂ습니다 / 습니까

‘ㅂ습니다 / 습니까’ attaches to a verb or an adjective to end a declarative sentence ‘-습니다’ or to ask a question ‘-습니까? in a formal situation.

When the verb or adjective stem ends with a consonant → -습니다.	When the verb or adjective stem ends with a vowel and a consonant ㄹ → -ㅂ니다.
있다: 있 + 습니다 → 있습니다 먹다: 먹 + 습니까 → 먹습니까? 귀엽다: 귀엽 + 습니다 → 귀엽습니다	가다: 가 + ㅂ니다 → 갑니다 예쁘다: 예쁘 + ㅂ니까 → 예쁩니까? 열다: 열 + ㅂ니다 → 엽니다 (In this case, the final consonant ㄹ will be dropped.)

사진을 찍습니다. I take a picture.

책을 읽습니다. I read a book.

만나서 반갑습니다. Nice to meet you.

공항에 갑니다. I go to the airport.

한국어를 공부합니까? Do you study Korean?

머리가 아픕니다. I have a headache.

🍀 **Change the following as shown in the example.**

Ex 보다 → 봅니다

(1) 읽다 → _____

(2) 자다 → _____

(3) 찾다 → _____

(4) 살다 → _____

Ex 쉬다 → 쉽니까?

(1) 있다 → _____ (2) 배우다 → _____

(3) 공부하다 → _____ (4) 열다 → _____

-입니다/입니까?

'입니다' is attached to a noun to form a predicative verb while '입니까?' is used to make questions. '입니다' and '입니까' are used in formal situations such as TV news, newspaper, and job interviews. They are also used to communicate with people of high rank or age.

입니다 / 입니까?
한국 사람 + 입니다 → 한국 사람입니다 대학생 + 입니까? → 대학생입니까?
A : 태국 사람입니까?　　　B : 아니요. 저는 한국 사람입니다. A: 대학생입니까?　　　　B: 아니요. 저는 회사원입니다.

저는 김민수입니다. I am Kim Minsoo. 　　학생입니까? Are you a student?

그것은 가방입니다. It's a bag. 　　이것은 무엇입니까? What's this?

알파 호텔입니다. This is the Alpha Hotel. 　여기가 어디입니까? Where are we?

🍀 **Create the dialogues as shown in the example.**

Ex (민수, 한국 사람)

A: 만나서 반갑습니다. 저는 민수입니다.

B: 반갑습니다. 민수 씨. 민수 씨는 한국 사람입니까?

A: 네, 저는 한국 사람입니다.

(1) (히엔, 베트남 사람)

A:_____

B:_____

A:_____

(2) (안나, 필리핀 사람)

A:_____

B:_____

A:_____

(3) (케이나, 캄보디아 사람)

A:_____

B:_____

A:_____

(4) (와차린, 태국 사람)

A:_____

B:_____

A:_____

-(으)시

'-(으)시' can be added to any verb stem in order to create it's honorific counterpart. Before you learn specifically when to add '~(으)시' to your sentences, let's remember when you should use honorifics in the first place. Remember, if you are talking to somebody who deserves a high level of respect, you should use honorifics. These types of people can be: bosses, parents, people older than you, guests, customers, etc. Therefore, the use of those honorifics solely depends on the person you are speaking to. The use of '~(으)시' is a little bit tricky at first. You should add '~(으)시' to verbs/adjectives in which the acting person deserves respect, regardless of who you are speaking to.

When the verb stem ends with a vowel and a consonant ㄹ → '-시'	When the verb stem ends with a consonant → '-으시
오다 : 오 + -시 → 오시다 살다 : 사 + -시 → 사시다 (The final consonant 'ㄹ' is dropped.)	읽다 : 읽 + -으시 → 읽으시다 듣다 : 들 + -으시 → 들으시다 (*ㄷ irregular)

아버지께서 내일 방콕에 오십니다. My father is coming to Bangkok tomorrow.

어머니께서 서울에 사십니다. My mother lives in Seoul.

선생님께서 책을 읽으십니다. The teacher reads a book.

할아버지께서 폭포 소리를 들으십니다. My grandfather hears the sound of a waterfall.

☞ **There are many words in the Korean language that have an honorific version. Below is a Korean honorifics list to help you get started.**

Dictionary Form	Honorific Form	Meaning
있다	계시다	To be somewhere or exist
먹다 / 마시다	드시다	To eat
자다	주무시다	To sleep

말하다	말씀하시다	To say or speak
죽다	돌아가시다	To die
아프다	편찮으시다	To be hurt, sick or in pain
주다	드리다	To give
묻다	여쭈다	To ask
배 고프다	시장하시다	To be hungry
데리고 가다	모시고 가다	To take someone somewhere

🍀 Change the following sentences as shown in the example.

> **Ex** 할머니께서 공항에 갑니다. → 할머니께서 공항에 가십니다.

(1) 사장님께서 전화를 합니다. → _____

(2) 어머니께서 한국어를 공부합니다. → _____

(3) 할아버지께서 방에서 잡니다. → _____

(4) 선생님께서 한국어를 너무 잘 가르칩니다. → _____

Track 2-03

A 지혜 씨는 어디에서 오셨어요? Where are you from, Jihye?

B 저는 한국에서 왔어요. I'm from Korea.

A 우진 씨도 한국에서 오셨어요? Woojin, are you also from Korea?

C 아니요, 저는 중국에서 왔어요. 중국 사람이에요. No, I'm from China. I'm Chinese.

A 아, 그래요? 실례했습니다. 모두 학생이세요? Oh, really? Excuse me. Are you all students?

B 네, 학생이에요. Yes, I'm a student

C 저는 학생이 아니에요. I'm not a student.

A 그럼, 우진 씨는 무슨 일을 하세요? Then, what do you do, Woojin?

C 은행에서 일합니다. 은행원입니다. I work at a bank. I'm a bank clerk.

A 아, 네. 부모님도 함께 오셨어요? Oh, yes. Did your parents come with you?

C 네, 가족 여행이에요. Yes, it's a family trip.

Key Grammar 핵심 문법

–에서

'–에서' is added to the end of location nouns to indicate that the preceding word refers to a place where a certain action is being done. It corresponds to 'at' or 'in' in English.

–에서
백화점 + 에서 → 백화점에서
커피숍 + 에서 → 커피숍에서

누나가 서울 백화점에서 쇼핑해요. My older sister shops at the Seoul department store.

형이 브라운 커피숍에서 커피를 마셔요. My brother drinks coffee at the Brown coffee shop.

친구가 편의점에서 일을 해요. My friend works at a convenient store.

❧ Create dialogues as shown in the example.

Ex A: 어디에서 친구를 만나요?

B: <u>공항에서 친구를 만나요.</u> (공항)

(1) A: 어디에서 저녁을 먹어요?

B: _____. (서울 식당)

(2) A: 어디에서 쇼핑해요?

B: _____. (센트럴 월드)

(3) A: 어디에서 공부해요?

B: _____. (도서관)

(4) A: 어디에서 커피를 마셔요?

B: _____. (스타벅스)

-도

'도' is a particle used after subject or object nouns to express the addition of a subject or object to one previously mentioned. It can replace subject or object markers and can be attached to '에' and '에서'. It corresponds to 'also', 'too', and 'even' in English.

-도	
친구 + 도 → 친구도 베트남에 + 도 → 베트남에도	한국어 + 도 → 한국어도 커피숍에서 + 도 → 커피숍에서도

저는 필리핀 사람이에요. 그리고 제 친구도 필리핀 사람이에요.

I'm Filipino. And my friend is also Filipino.

저는 영어를 잘 해요. 그리고 한국어도 잘 해요.

I am good at English. And I am also good at Korean.

캄보디아에 친구가 있어요. 그리고 베트남에도 친구가 있어요.

I have a friend in Cambodia. And I also have a friend in Vietnam.

도서관에서 책을 봐요. 그리고 커피숍에서도 책을 봐요.

I read books in the library. And I read books at the coffee shop, too.

♣ **Create the dialogue using '도' as shown in the example.**

Ex A: 과일을 좋아해요?

B: 네, 사과를 좋아해요. 그리고 배도 좋아해요. (사과 + 배)

(1) A: 부모님이 키가 커요?

B: _____. (아버지 + 어머니)

(2) A: 마이클 씨는 뭘 잘해요?

B: _____. (공부 + 운동)

(3) A: 가방에 뭐가 있어요?

B: _____. (여권 + 지갑)

(4) A: 지난 휴가 때 어디에 갔어요?

B: _____. (태국 + 캄보디아)

무슨

'무슨' is placed before nouns to express either 'what' or 'what kind of' in English. You'll also hear sentences like '무슨 소리야?' which literally translates to "what noise is it?" but really means "what are you saying?" It's used when someone says some nonsense or something ridiculous.

무슨
무슨 + 영화 → 무슨 영화
무슨 + 책 → 무슨 책

무슨 영화를 보고 싶어요? What movie do you want to see?

무슨 책을 읽어요? What book are you reading?

무슨 드라마를 좋아해요? What drama do you like?

♣ **Complete the following sentences using '무슨' as shown in the example.**

> Ex A: 무슨 꽃을 좋아해요?   B: 장미를 좋아해요.

(1) A : _____ 마셔요?   B: 홍차를 마셔요.

(2) A : _____ 먹어요?   B: 김치찌개를 먹어요.

(3) A : _____ 사요?   B: 망고를 사요.

(4) A : _____ 좋아해요?   B: 축구를 좋아해요.

–이/가 아니다

'아닙니다' is honorific version of '아니다' while '아니다' is the negative form of '이다'. '이/가 아닙니다' is used after a noun to indicate that the noun is not correct as stated in a formal situation. It is the negative form of '입니다'. '이/가 아닙니까' is used to form questions.

Nouns ending with a vowel → 가 아닙니다	Nouns ending with a consonant → 이 아닙니다
관광가이드 + 가 아닙니다 → 관광가이드가 아닙니다	한국 사람 + 이 아닙니다 → 한국 사람이 아닙니다

저분은 수잔 씨가 아닙니다. That person is not Susan.

저는 태국 사람이 아닙니다. I am not a Thai.

이것은 볼펜이 아닙니다. This is not a ballpoint pen.

♣ Fill in the blanks as shown in the example.

> **Ex** A: 필리핀 사람입니까?
> B: 네, <u>필리핀 사람입니다.</u>
>
> A: 학생입니까?
> B: 아니요, <u>학생이 아닙니다.</u>

(1) A: 한국 사람입니까?　　　　　B: _____. 한국 사람이 아닙니다.

(2) A: 사과는 과일입니까?　　　　B: 네, _____.

(3) A: 마이클 씨는 선생님입니까?　B: 아니요. _____.

(4) A: 수민 씨는 간호사입니까?　　B: _____, 수민 씨는 간호사가 아닙니다.

4 Response Exercise 응답 연습

(First and last greetings 처음과 끝 인사

Track 2-04

When meeting someone for the first time or greeting someone you know but need to speak to politely, bow your head to indicate respect.

> **A** 안녕하세요? Hello.
>
> **B** 안녕하세요? Hello.

When meeting someone of higher status, or with whom you have a working relationship.

> **A** 안녕하십니까? How do you do?
>
> **B** 안녕하십니까? How do you do?

When a person stays, he/she says "안녕히 가세요" to the person who leaves. When a person leaves, he/she says "안녕히 계세요" to the person who stays.

A 안녕히 가세요. Goodbye.

B 안녕히 계세요. Goodbye.

The polite and formal versions of the greeting '안녕히 가세요' / '안녕히 계세요' are as follows:

A 안녕히 가십시오. Goodbye.

B 안녕히 계십시오. Goodbye.

Morning greetings 아침 인사

Track 2-05

A 안녕하세요? 좋은 아침입니다. Hello, good morning.

B 네, 안녕하세요? Yes, hello.

A 안녕하세요? 편히 주무셨어요? Hello? Did you have a good sleep?

B 네, 잘 잤어요. 안녕하세요? Yes, I had a good sleep. Hello?

A 안녕하세요? 상쾌한 아침이에요. Hello? It's a refreshing morning.

B 네, 감사합니다. 잘 주무셨어요? Yes, thank you. Did you sleep well?

Greetings in the evening 저녁 인사

Track 2-06

A 안녕히 주무세요. Good night.

B 네, 안녕히 주무세요. Yes, good night.

A 편안한 저녁 보내세요. Have a pleasant evening.

B 네, 안녕히 주무세요. Yes, good night.

A 편안한 밤 보내시고 내일 뵙겠습니다. Have a pleasant night and see you tomorrow.

B 오늘도 수고 많으셨습니다. 감사합니다. You did a really good job today. Thank you.

A 오늘 고생 많으셨어요. 조심히 들어가세요. Thank you for your hard work today. Be careful on your way back home.

B 감사합니다. 내일 뵐게요. Thank you. I'll see you tomorrow.

Other greetings 그 밖의 인사

Track 2-07

When expressing gratitude politely in a formal situation:

A 감사합니다. Thank you.

B 천만예요. You're welcome.

When expressing apology politely in a formal situation:

A 미안합니다. I'm sorry.

B 아니요, 괜찮습니다. No, that's all right.

When expressing apology politely in an informal situation:

A 죄송합니다. I'm sorry.

B 아니에요, 괜찮아요. No, it's okay.

When you want to ask something:

A 실례하겠습니다. Excuse me.

B 네, 괜찮습니다. Yes, it's fine. / I don't mind.

5 Pronunciation 발음

Final consonant Rule (받침 규칙)

Track 2-08

Korean alphabet consonants have their sound values in the syllable initial position. When they are located in the syllable final position, only seven sounds, [-k](ㄱ, ㄲ, ㅋ, ㄺ), [-n](ㄴ, ㄶ, ㄵ), [-t](ㄷ, ㅅ, ㅆ, ㅈ, ㅊ, ㅌ, ㅎ), [-l](ㄹ, ㄼ), [-m](ㅁ, ㄻ), [-p](ㅂ, ㅍ, ㅄ), [-ŋ](ㅇ) are represented.

Ex 부엌 → [부억] 밖 → [박] 맑다 → [막따] 앉고 → [안꼬] 듣다 → [듣따] 낮 → [낟]
옷 → [옫] 몇 → [멷] 밑 → [믿] 넓게 → [널께] 젊고 → [점꼬] 앞 → [압]
없다 → [업따]

When ㄷ, ㅌ, ㅅ, ㅆ, ㅈ, ㅊ, or ㅎ appears as a final consonant, they are all represent as [ㄷ]. In the example above, the final consonant 'ㅆ' in '겠' is pronounced as [ㄷ] as [ㄷ] is the representative sound of the final consonants, 'ㅅ, ㅈ, ㅊ, ㅌ, ㅎ, ㅆ'.

Ex 빗 → [빋] 빚 → [빋] 빛 → [빋] 닫다 → [닫따] 솥 → [솓] 있다 → [읻따] 꽃 → [꼳]
히읗 → [히읃]

6 Additional Expression 추가 표현

A	■ 이름이 뭐예요? What is your name?
	❏ 실례지만, 성함이 어떻게 되세요? Excuse me, what's your name?
B	저는 김영수예요. I'm Kim Youngsoo.
	[제 이름은 김영수입니다.] [My name is Kim Youngsoo.]
	[저는 김영수라고 합니다.] [My name is Kim Youngsoo.]

A	■ 직업이 어떻게 되세요? What do you do for a living?
	❏ 실례지만, 직업이 뭐예요? Excuse me, what do you do for a living?

B	저는 은행원이에요. I work as a bank clerk.
	[제 직업은 은행원입니다.] [My job is a bank clerk.]
	[저는 은행에서 일해요.] [I work at a bank.]
	[저는 은행에 다닙니다.] [I work at a bank.]

7 Culture of Korea

7.1 한국의 언어 문화

Responding to what someone says:

- 아, 그래요? Oh, it is? / Oh, really?
- 네, 그렇습니까? Is that so?
- 그렇군요. Right.

Expressing "thank you" in most everyday situations:

Although both '고맙습니다' and '감사합니다' are used interchangeably, it's easier to find '감사합니다' in formal occasions whereas '고맙습니다' is more common for daily usage. Note that '감사하다' is a verb and also an adjective while '고맙다' is only an adjective.

- 고맙습니다. Thank you.
- 감사합니다. Thank you.

Expressing apology to someone：

"미안합니다" is used in semi-formal situations when the person in the same or lower position is on the other side, and "죄송합니다" is used in more formal situations when the upper person is on the other side.

- 미안합니다. I'm sorry.
- 죄송합니다. I'm sorry.

7.2 한국인의 인사와 호칭

Ways of Addressing and Greeting Korean Tourists
한국인의 인사와 다른 사람을 부를 때 호칭

How should someone address and greet Korean tourists when meeting them for the first time? In some cases, some countries greet each other differently in the morning, afternoon, and evening, but Koreans usually use 'Hello?' the most regardless of time. In order to make a good first impression on Koreans, it is very important to use Korean-style greetings and titles that suit the situation and the other person.

What would be an appropriate way of addressing the person you meet? In this situation, it is necessary to check the names of Koreans. Korean names consist of two parts: a family name, a first name, and a given name. Most Koreans have a one-syllable surname and a two-syllable name. If you meet a person with whom you have a business relationship, you can add a title or position after his/her full name, such as "(full name) president" or "(full name) manager," and put "nim [님]" at the end to show respect.

However, Koreans usually add "Ssi [씨]" to the person's full name or the given name. For example, if the last name is "Kim" and the given name is "Hojun," he is addressed as "Kim

Hojun Ssi" or "Hojun Ssi." In this case, it would be rude to address an older person or a person with a higher position by his/her first name or 'last name + Ssi'. Even if the other person is young, it may be rude to address him/her as "you" or his/her name unless you have a close relationship with him/her. So, be careful.

How should someone greet in Korean? Koreans bow down first when they meet someone. At this time, the greeting is a little different depending on the person you meet. If that person is older, it requires you to be polite, so bow deeply. When meeting someone for the first time, Koreans usually say this, "Hello? It's a great pleasure to meet you. I'm ⋯." revealing his/her name (including his/her position or title). As a response, the other person says, "Yes, hello. It's a great pleasure to meet you too. I'm ⋯." However, if the other person is a friend or someone with a close relationship, they sometimes bow their heads lightly or wave their hands. In the case of men, there are many people who shake hands in a western way. In this case, it would be rude for a subordinate to ask for a handshake first, so you should be careful.

When greeting Korean tourists in the morning on the second day and the succeeding mornings of their stay, you can say, 'Did you sleep well?', "Did you sleep comfortably?" and "Did you have breakfast?" At the end of the day's tour, you can also express your friendliness and gratitude with closing remarks such as "Did you have fun today?", "You did very well", and "Thank you. Please rest well."

Answers

(1) 는   (2) 은   (3) 은   (4) 는

(1) 이에요.   (2) 예요.   (3) 예요.   (4) 이에요.

(1) 가요.   (2) 넓어요.   (3) 먹어요.   (4) 전화해요.

Answers

(1) 읽습니다.   (2) 잡습니다.   (3) 찾습니다.   (4) 삽니다.

(1) 있습니까?   (2) 배웁니까?   (3) 공부합니까?   (4) 엽니까?

(1) A : 만나서 반갑습니다. 저는 히엔입니다.

    B : 반갑습니다. 히엔 씨. 히엔 씨는 베트남 사람입니까?

    A : 네, 저는 베트남 사람입니다.

(2) A : 만나서 반갑습니다. 저는 안나입니다.

    B : 반갑습니다. 안나 씨. 안나 씨는 필리핀 사람입니까?

    A : 네, 저는 필리핀 사람입니다.

(3) A : 만나서 반갑습니다. 저는 케이나입니다.

    B : 반갑습니다. 케이나 씨. 케이나 씨는 캄보디아 사람입니까?

    A : 네, 저는 캄보디아 사람입니다.

(4) A : 만나서 반갑습니다. 와차린입니다.

    B : 반갑습니다. 와차란 씨. 와차린 씨는 태국 사람입니까?

    A : 네, 저는 태국 사람입니다.

(1) 제인 씨가 전화를 하십니다.

(2) 어머니께서 한국어를 공부하십니다.

(3) 할아버지께서 방에서 주무십니다.

(4) 선생님께서 한국어를 너무 잘 가르치십니다.

(1) 서울 식당에서 저녁을 먹어요.　　(2) 센트럴 월드에서 쇼핑해요.

(3) 도서관에서 공부해요.　　(4) 스타벅스에서 커피를 마셔요.

(1) 아버지가 키가 커요. 그리고 어머니도 키가 커요.

(2) 공부를 잘 해요. 그리고 운동도 잘 해요.

(3) 여권이 있어요. 그리고 지갑도 있어요.

(4) 태국에 갔어요. 그리고 캄보디아에도 갔어요.

(1) 무슨 차를　　(2) 무슨 찌개를　　(3) 무슨 과일을　　(4) 무슨 운동을

(1) 아니요.　　(2) 과일입니다.　　(3) 선생님이 아닙니다.　　(4) 아니요.

메모

3

실례지만 여권 좀 보여 주세요
Excuse me, but please show me your passport

Unit 3

실례지만 여권 좀 보여 주세요
Excuse me, but please show me your passport

✎ To know expression common in room reservation, accommodation, and hotel (호텔과 숙박 예약)

✎ To check-in and check-out (체크인과 체크아웃)

✎ To familiarize vocabulary related to hotel services and facilities (호텔 서비스와 시설 이용)

✎ To solve complaints and problems from hotel guests (호텔 고객의 불편)

2 Vocabulary 어휘

2.1 Dialogue Vocabulary 본문 어휘

<u>Noun</u> 명사 ✎

여권 passport	호실 room number	체크아웃 check-out
체크인 check-in	계산서 check / bill	애플 페이 Apple Pay
분 person (honorific)	달러 dollar	사인 signature
가방 bag	레스토랑 restaurant	날짜 date

수요일 Wednesday   오후 afternoon / p.m.   7시 seven o'clock

그 날 that day   저녁 evening   단체 group

목요일 Thursday   테라스 terrace   자리 seat

이름 name   손님 guest

성함 name (honorific)   전화번호 phone number

Verb 동사 ✏️

돕다 help   주다/드리다 give (honorific)   실례하다 excuse oneself

있다 exist / there is   기다리다 wait   해 드리다 do as a favor

계산하다 count payment   되다 become   맡기다 leave

안내하다 guide   알려주다 inform   예약하다 reserve

가능하다 It's possible   죄송하다 I'm sorry   받다 receive

확인하다 confirm

Others 나머지 ✏️

무엇 What   좀 please / a little   여기 here

잠시 for a moment   어떻게 how   모두 altogether

그리고 and   물론 of course   바로 immediately

언제 when   다른 different   그래요 Yeah

그럼 then   지금 now

2.2 Related Vocabulary 관련 어휘

호텔서비스와 시설 이용 Use of Hotel Services and Facilities

예약자 person who made reservation		3박 three nights
객실 room / cabin	열쇠 key	계산 counting payment
알람 시계 alarm clock	청구서 bill / check	프런트 데스크 front desk
방 room	호 number	예약 reservation
싱글룸 single room	트윈룸 twin room	더블룸 double room
침구 bedding	에어컨 air conditioner	일정 schedule
지연 delay	추가 요금 additional charge	보여주다 show
맡기다 leave	묵다 stay	변경하다 change
바꾸다 change	부탁하다 ask	지불하다 pay
부탁드리다 ask (honorific)	추가하다 add	가져다 드리다 bring
좋다 good / fine / nice	어렵다 difficult	틀리다 incorrect /wrong
쉽다 easy	괜찮다 It's okay	알겠습니다 I see

때와 상황 Time and Situations

어제 yesterday	내일 tomorrow	모레 the day after tomorrow
때 time / moment	시간 time	취침 시간 bedtime
정시 on time	오전 a.m.	1일 a day
오늘밤 tonight	작년 last year	올해/금년 this year
내년 next year	곧 right away	한번에 at once
언제든지 anytime	일찍 early	
매년 yearly / annually / every year		

Dialogue 1 **Check-in** 체크인

Track 3-01

A 안녕하세요. 무엇을 도와 드릴까요? Hello. May I help you?

B 체크인을 하고 싶어요. 제 이름은 김민수예요.
I'd like to check in. My name is Kim Min-soo.

A 네, 알겠습니다. 실례지만 여권 좀 보여주세요.
Yes, sir. Excuse me, can I see your passport?

B 네, 여기 있어요. Sure, here you are.

Key Grammar 핵심 문법

-(으)ㄹ까요?

'-(으)ㄹ까요?' is used to suggest the listener doing something together or ask the listener's choice regarding something; corresponding to 'Shall we ~, why don't we ~" in English. It is also used to make a suggestion to the lister or ask the listener's opinion regarding something; corresponding to 'Shall I ~, Should I ~' in English. In response, although the same verb as the one used in original suggestion can be used with the ending '-ㅂ시다', the pattern '좋아요' and '그럽시다' are more natural.

Verb stem ending with a vowel or ㄹ → ㄹ까요?	Verb stem ending with a consonant → 을까요?
드리다: 드리 + ㄹ까요? → 드릴까요? 열다: 열 + ㄹ까요? → 열까요? (* ㄹ is dropped from the verb stem.)	먹다: 먹 + 을까요? → 먹을까요? 걷다: 걷 + 을까요? → 걸을까요? (* ㄷ irregular verb)

이거 드릴까요? Shall I give you this?

창문을 열까요? Shall I open the window?

오늘 점심에 뭐 먹을까요? What shall we eat for lunch today?

우리 호텔까지 걸을까요? Shall we walk to the hotel?

♣ **Use the words in parentheses to complete the following dialogues as in the example.**

> Ex A: 같이 <u>영화를 볼까요?</u> (영화를 보다)   B : 네, <u>봐요</u>.

(1) A: 같이 _____? (여행을 가다)   B: _____.

(2) A: 같이 _____? (책을 읽다)   B: _____.

(3) A : 같이 _____? (밥을 먹다)   B: _____.

(4) A : 같이 _____? (노래를 부르다)   B: _____.

–고 싶다

'–고 싶다' expresses the wish or hope of the speaker and corresponds to 'want to' in English. If the subject is in the first or second person, then '–고 싶다' is used. When the subject is in the third person, then '–고 싶어하다' is used.

–고 싶다
가다: 가 + 고 싶다 → 가고 싶다 받다: 받 + 고 싶다 → 받고 싶다

저는 BTS 콘서트에 가고 싶어요. I want to go to the BTS concert.

생일에 예쁜 지갑을 받고 싶어요. I want to get a pretty wallet for my birthday.

제 친구도 BTS 콘서트에 가고 싶어해요. My friend also wants to go to the BTS concert.

♣ **Complete the following sentences using** '–고 싶어요' **as in the example.**

Ex 커피를 마시다 → 커피를 마시고 싶어요

(1) 선물을 받다 → _____.

(2) 휴대폰을 사다 → _____.

(3) 쇼핑을 하다 → _____.

(4) 한국어를 잘 하다 → _____.

-아/어/여 주세요

'-아/어/여 주세요' expresses a request to someone to perform an action and corresponds to 'Please ~, Would you ~' in English. '-아/어/여 주시겠어요?' is a more polite expression that shows more consideration for the listener than '-아/어/여 주세요'.

-아 주세요 is attached to stem ending in the vowels ㅏ or ㅗ.	-어 주세요 is attached to stems ending in other vowels.	-해 주세요 is attached to stem ending in -하다.
닫다: 닫 + -아 주세요 → 닫아 주세요	읽다: 읽 + -어 주세요 → 읽어 주세요	청소하다: 청소 + -해 주세요 → 청소해 주세요

문을 닫아 주세요. Please close the door.

방을 청소해 주세요. Please clean the room.

책을 읽어 주세요. Please read the book

가방을 들어 주시겠어요? Would you please carry my bag for me? (More polite expression)

☞ If someone asks you for a favor and you are willing to comply, you can reply using '-아/어/여 드리겠습니다'.

A 예약이 확인되면 연락해 주시겠어요?
Would you please contact me once the reservation is confirmed?

B 네, 전화해 드리겠습니다. Yes, I'll give you a call.

🍀 **Fill in the blanks using** '아/어/여 주세요' **as shown in the example.**

Ex 천천히 이야기하다 → 천천히 이야기해 주세요

(1) 책을 찾다 → _____.

(2) 조용히 하다 → _____.

(3) 문법을 가르치다 → _____.

(4) 문을 열다 → _____.

🍀 Change the following sentences as shown in the example.

> **Ex** 모레 저녁으로 예약해 주세요. → <u>모레 저녁으로 예약해 주시겠어요?</u>

(1) 좀 더 기다려 주세요. → _____

(2) 내일 아침에 전화해 주세요. → _____

(3) 천천히 말씀해 주세요. → _____

(4) 이것 좀 치워 주세요. → _____

-지만

'지만' is attached after a verb stem or an adjective stem to connect two words or sentences when the following word or sentence is different from the preceding word or sentence. It corresponds to 'but' in English. In case of the past tense, '-았/었지만' is attached.

-지만
작다: 작 + 지만 → 작지만 비싸다: 비싸 + 지만 → 비싸지만 왔다: 왔 + 지만 → 왔지만

딸기는 작지만 수박은 커요. Strawberries are small, but watermelons are big.

불고기는 비싸지만 맛있어요. Bulgogi is expensive but delicious.

어제는 비가 왔지만 오늘은 날씨가 맑아요.

It rained yesterday, but the weather is clear today.

♣ Connect the following sentences as shown in the example.

> Ex 푸엉은 베트남 사람이다 / 한국말을 잘 하다
> → 푸엉은 베트남 사람이지만 한국말을 잘 해요.

(1) 김치는 맵다 / 맛있다

→ _____

(2) 휴대 전화가 예쁘다 / 비싸다

→ _____

(3) 한국어 공부는 어렵다 / 재미있다

→ _____

(4) 겨울은 춥다 / 여름은 덥다

→ _____

Dialogue 2 **Check-out** 체크 아웃

Track 3-02

A 안녕하세요? 도와 드릴까요? Hello? May I help you?

B 네, 304호실 체크아웃을 하고 싶어요. Yes, I'd like to check out room 304.

A 네, 잠시만 기다려 주세요. 여기, 계산서입니다
Yes, please wait a moment. Here's the bill.

계산은 어떻게 해 드릴까요? How would you like to pay?

B 제가 애플 페이로 계산하고 싶어요. I'd like to pay with Apple Pay.

A 네, 됩니다. 모두 164달러입니다. Yes, you can. It's 164 dollars in total.

계산서에 사인해 주시겠어요? Could you sign the bill, please?

B 여기요. 그리고 잠시 가방 좀 맡기고 싶어요. 괜찮을까요?
Here it is. And I'd like to leave my bag with you for a while. Will it be okay?

A 네, 물론입니다. 바로 안내해 드리겠습니다.
Yes, of course. I'll show you right away.

B 고맙습니다. Thank you.

Key Grammar 핵심 문법

−이/가

'이/가' is a subject marker indicating that the noun it is attached to is the subject of the sentence. If a noun ends with a vowel, '가' is added.

Nouns ending with a vowel → 가	Nouns ending with a consonant → 이
환전소 + 가 → 환전소가	공항 + 이 → 공항이

환전소가 어디예요? Where is the currency exchange?

망고가 맛있어요. Mango is delicious.   공항이 멀어요. The airport is far away.

저기가 식당이에요. That's the restaurant.   제 가방이 무거워요. My bag is heavy.

♣ Complete the sentences as shown in the example.

> **Ex** 한국어 공부 / 재미있다 → <u>한국어 공부가 재미있어요.</u>

(1) 비빔밥 / 맛있다 → _____

(2) 자동차 / 많다 → _____

(3) 지하철 / 빠르다 → _____

(4) 제임스 씨 / 밥을 먹다 → _____

–(으)로[1]

'(으)로' attaches after a noun and indicates a method, means, and tool of action. It corresponds to 'by', 'with' or 'using' in English.

Nouns ending with a vowel or ㄹ → 로	Nouns ending with a consonant → 으로
신용카드 + 로 신용카드로	젓가락 + 으로 → 젓가락으로

신용카드로 결제하고 싶어요. I'd like to pay by credit card.

문을 열쇠로 잠그세요. Please lock the door with a key.

길이 막히니까 택시로 가세요. Please take a taxi because there's a traffic jam.

한국 사람은 젓가락으로 반찬을 먹어요. Koreans eat side dishes with chopsticks.

휴대폰으로 비행기표를 예매했어요. I booked a plane ticket on my cell phone.

입국 서류는 볼펜으로 쓰세요. Please write your entry documents with a ballpoint pen.

🍀 Answer the following questions as shown in the example.

Ex A: 어떻게 짐을 보내실 거예요?   B: (비행기) 비행기로 보내 주세요.

(1) A: 공항에 어떻게 갈 거예요?   B: (택시) _____

(2) A: 요금을 어떻게 지불하시겠어요?   B: (현금) _____

(3) A: 국수를 어떻게 먹어요?   B: (젓가락) _____

(4) A: 한국어 공부를 어떻게 해요?   B: (유튜브) _____

-겠

'-겠' is added to the verb stem to express the intention or will of the speaker. It corresponds to 'will/am going to ~' or 'plan to ~' in English. It can also be used to convey information that something is about to occur. In this case, it corresponds to 'should' or 'will' in English.

−겠
사다: 사 + 겠 → 사겠어요 끊다: 끊 + 겠 → 끊겠어요 하다: 하 + 겠 → 하겠어요

오늘 점심은 제가 사겠습니다. I'll treat you to lunch today.

오늘부터 담배를 끊겠습니다. I'll quit smoking from today.

올해에는 열심히 공부하겠어요. I will study hard this year.

☞ The negative form is made by adding '−지 않겠어요' ['−지 않겠습니다'] or '안 −겠어요' ['안 −겠습니다'].

더 이상 담배를 피우지 않겠어요 [않겠습니다]. I won't smoke a cigarette any more.

🍀 **Fill in the blanks using** '겠습니다' **as shown in the example.**

> **Ex** 올해에는 담배를 꼭 끊다 → 올해에는 담배를 꼭 끊겠습니다.

(1) 아침에 운동하다 → _____.

(2) 저는 비빔밥을 먹다 → _____.

(3) 제가 커피를 사 오다 → _____.

(4) 예약을 확인해 드리다 → _____.

Track 3-03

A 호텔 레스토랑 데메테르입니다. 무엇을 도와드릴까요?
This is the hotel restaurant Demeter. How may I help you?

B 여보세요? 예약을 하고 싶어요. Hello? I'd like to make a reservation.

A 네, 언제 날짜로 해 드릴까요? Yes, what date would you like to do?

B 10월 9일 수요일 오후 7시로 가능할까요?
Is it possible for 7 p.m. on Wednesday, October 9th?

A 죄송하지만 그 날 저녁은 예약을 안 받습니다. 단체 예약이 있습니다.
I'm sorry, but we don't accept reservations for that evening. We have a group reservation.

다른 날짜를 확인해 드릴까요? Do you want me to check another date?

B 그래요? 그럼 10월 10일 목요일 오후 7시로 예약 가능할까요?
Really? Then can I make a reservation for Thursday, October 10th at 7 pm?

A 네, 가능합니다. 지금 예약을 해 드릴까요?
Yes, it's possible. Would you like me to make a reservation now?

B 네, 해 주세요. 죄송하지만 테라스 자리로 예약해 주시겠어요?
Yes, please go ahead. I'm sorry, but could you reserve a terrace seat?

A 알겠습니다. 어느 분 이름으로 예약해 드릴까요?
I see. Under whose name should I make a reservation?

B 저예요. It's me.

A 네, 손님 성함과 전화번호를 알려 주시겠습니까?
Yes, may I have your name and phone number?

Key Grammar 핵심 문법

Time and Date 시간과 날짜 ▶

Counting Systems in Korean 숫자 체계

Number systems are used to count numbers, money and other objects in Korean. Koreans use two different number systems, namely Native Korean system and Sino Korean system depending on the objects being counted.

Sino Korean number system

0 영 1 일 2 이 3 삼 4 사 5 오 6 육 7 칠 8 팔 9 구 10 십

11 십일 12 십이 13 십삼 14 십사 15 십오 16 십육 17 십칠 18 십팔 19 십구 20 이십

30 삼십 40 사십 50 오십 60 육십 70 칠십 80 팔십 90 구십 100 백 200 이백 300 삼백

1,000 천 2,000 이천 10,000 만 20,000 이만 1,000,000 백만 100,000,000 억

1000,000,000,000 조

🍀 **Count numbers as shown in the example.**

Ex 27 (이십칠)　89 (팔십구)　600 (육백)　118 (백십팔)　542 (오백사십이)

1,234 (천이백삼십사)　2,500 (이천오백)　7,539 (칠천오백삼십구)　40,000 (사만)

87,654 (팔만칠천육백오십사)　3,000,000 (삼백만)　10,000,000 (천만)

87,000,000 (팔천칠백만)　50,953,289 (오천구십오만삼천이백팔십구)

(1) 83 (   )   (2) 749 (   )   (3) 3,195 (   )

(4) 4,700 (   )   (5) 600,000 (   )   (6) 5,290,100 (   )

Native Korean number system

1 하나 2 둘 3 셋 4 넷 5 다섯 6 여섯 7 일곱 8 여덟 9 아홉 10 열 11 열하나
12 열둘 20 스물 21 스물하나 22 스물둘 30 서른 40 마흔 50 쉰 60 예순 70 일흔
80 여든 90 아흔

Note that adjective forms of 하나, 둘, 셋, 넷 and 스물 are 한, 두, 세, 네 and 스무. The choice of noun and adjective depends only on the last syllable while all other syllables remain in the noun form even when the numbers are used as an adjective.

	Noun Form	Adjective Form
11	열하나	열한
20	스물	스무
22	스물둘	스물두
33	서른셋	서른세
44	마흔넷	마흔네
55	쉰다섯	쉰다섯
66	예순여섯	예순여섯

Dates 날짜

The dates are written in the order of year(년), month(월), and day(일) in Korean. For example, today is the 6th of March, 2022. Then it's written as 2022년 3월 6일 (이천이십이년 삼월 육일). To express the dates, Sino Korean numbers are used.

일월 January   이월 February   삼월 March   사월 April   오월 May   유월 June

칠월 July   팔월 August   구월 September   시월 October   십일월 November
십이월 December

어린이날은 오월 오일이에요. Children's Day falls on May 5th.

한글날은 시월 구일이에요. Hangeul Day is 9th of October.

크리스마스는 십이월 이십오일이에요. Christmas falls on the 25th of December.

Days of the week 요일

월요일 Monday   화요일 Tuesday   수요일 Wednesday   목요일 Thursday   금요일 Friday
토요일 Saturday   일요일 Sunday

A: 오늘 무슨 요일이에요? What day is it today?

B: 오늘은 일요일이에요. Today is Sunday.

A: 우리 언제 만나요? When do we meet?

B: 수요일에 만나요. See you on Wednesday.

As an alternate to counting days using 일일, 이일, 삼일 etc, we can also use the following traditional system when counting the number of days as a duration.

하루 one day, 이틀 two days, 사흘 three days, 나흘 four days, 닷새 five days, 엿새 six days, 이레 seven days, 여드레 eight days, 아흐레 nine days, 열흘 ten days

내 생일이 이틀 남았어요. It is two days before my birthday

이 호텔에 닷새 동안 머물 거예요. I'm staying at this hotel for five days.

하루 전에 예약을 하세요. Make a reservation a day in advance.

Hours and Minutes 시와 분

When telling the hours, the Native Korean number is used with the counting unit being '시'.
On the other hand, the Sino Korean number is used to say the minutes, '분'.

☞ Korean also has a word for "half past" (i.e., 5:30), which is '반'. This means "half" in Korean. It makes things a bit simpler when reading the time.

🍀 Express the time as shown in the example.

> **Ex** 3:27 a.m. (오전 세시 이십칠분)
> 8:30 p.m. (오후 여덟시 삼십분 / 오후 여덟시 반)

(1) 3:24 p.m. _____ (2) 7:36 a.m. _____

(3) 12:30 a.m. _____ (4) 1:55 p.m. _____

안 + verb/adjective, verb/adjective + 지 않다

'안' refers to one's unwillingness and expresses the meaning of 'does not' or 'is not'. It applies more to the speaker's intention and conscious choice. '안 + Verb/Adjectiv' the rule for putting a verb or adjective is very simple. Just add '안' immediately before verbs and adjectives.

안–
마시다: 안 + 마시다 → 안 마시다
좋다: 안 + 좋다 → 안 좋다
맵다: 안 + 맵다 → 안 맵다

저녁에는 커피를 안 마셔요. I don't drink coffee in the evening.

오늘은 날씨가 안 좋아요. The weather is bad today.

이 김치는 안 매워요. This kimchi is not spicy.

☞ For 하다 verbs, which consist of nouns and 하다, 안 goes between the noun and 하다.

공부하다: 공부 + 안 + 하다 → 공부 안 하다

일하다: 일 + 안 + 하다 → 일 안 하다

저는 밤 11시 이후에는 공부 안 해요. I don't study after 11 p.m.

우체국 직원들은 주말에 일 안 해요. Post office workers don't work on weekends.

식사 후에는 운동을 안 해요. I don't exercise after meal.

---

verb/adjective + 지 않다

The second way to make negation is to put '–지 않다' right after verbs and adjectives. You can use this form with any verbs and adjectives. Just take the verb or adjective stem and attach '–지 않다'.

–지 않다
가다: 가 + 지 않다 → 가지 않다
먹다: 먹 + 지 않다 → 먹지 않다
춥다: 춥 + 지 않다 → 춥지 않다

토요일에는 학교를 가지 않아요. I don't go to school on Saturdays.

제임스 씨는 김치를 먹지 않아요. James doesn't eat kimchi.

이번 겨울은 춥지 않아요. It's not cold this winter.

🍀 Complete the sentences as shown in the example.

> **Ex** 제임스 씨는 이번에 휴가를 <u>안 가요</u>. (가다 X)
> 제임스 씨는 이번에 휴가를 <u>가지 않아요.</u>

(1) 오늘은 별로 _____. (덥다 X)
 오늘은 별로 _____.

(2) 술을 마셔서 _____. (운전하다 X)
 술을 마셔서 _____.

(3) 재래시장은 물건이 _____. (비싸다 X)
 재래시장은 물건이 _____.

(4) 한국어 수업이 _____. (어렵다 X)
 한국어 수업이 _____.

4 Response Exercise 응답 연습

Check-in 체크인

Track 3-04

A 체크인을 하고 싶은데요. I'd like to check in.
 [예약을 했는데요, 체크인 하고 싶어요.] [I have a reservation and so I'd like to check in.]

B 네, 알겠습니다. Yes, sir / Ma'am.
 먼저 오신 분부터 하고 바로 해 드리겠습니다.
 I'll start with the guest who came first and do it right away.

A 전망 좋은 방에서 묵고 싶어요.
 I want to stay in a room with a nice view.

B 죄송합니다만 예약이 가득 차서 어렵겠습니다.
I'm sorry, but it'll be difficult because it's full

[죄송하지만 전망 좋은 방은 다 찼습니다.]
[I'm sorry, but the rooms with a good view are all booked.]

A 예약은 안 했습니다만 지금 빈 방이 있어요?
I didn't make a reservation, but do you have any vacant rooms now?

B 네, 빈 객실이 좀 있습니다. Yes, we have some vacant rooms.

A 금연룸, 흡연룸 중 어느 방으로 드릴까요?
Would you like a non-smoking room or a smoking room?

B 금연룸으로 주세요. I'd like a non-smoking room, please.

Check-Out 체크 아웃

Track 3-05

A 저희 호텔에서 편안하셨습니까? Did you feel comfortable in our hotel?
[저희 숙소에서 즐거운 시간을 보내셨나요?] [Did you have a great time at our hotel?]

B 네, 덕분에 편하게 있었습니다. Yes, thanks to you, I had a comfortable stay.
머무는 동안 정말 즐거웠어요. I really enjoyed staying while I'm here.

A 몇 시에 체크아웃 해야 합니까? What time should I check out?

B 12시 전에 체크아웃 하셔야 합니다. You have to check out before 12 o'clock.

A 하루 일찍 체크아웃 하고 싶은데요. I'd like to check out a day earlier.

B 계산서를 준비해 드리겠습니다. I'll prepare the bill for you.

A 하루 더 묵을 수 있을까요? Can I stay one more day?

B 죄송하지만 예약이 다 찼습니다. I'm sorry, but we're fully booked.

Response and guidance to inquiries about hotel facilities
호텔 시설 이용 문의에 대한 응답 및 안내 답변

Track 3-06

A 여기 1209호실이에요. 와이파이가 안 돼요.
This is room 1209. The Wi-Fi isn't working.

[TV가 안 나와요.] [The TV isn't working.]

[옆 방 손님들이 너무 시끄러워요.]
[The guests in the next room are making too much noise.]

B 알겠습니다. 지금 바로 확인해 드리겠습니다. Okay. I'll check it right away.

[네, 지금 사람을 보내 확인해 드리겠습니다.

[Yes, I'm now sending someone to check.]

[알겠습니다. 저희가 조치해 드리겠습니다.] [I'm on it, we'll take care of it.]

A 여기 1209호실이에요. 짐을 운반할 사람을 보내 주시겠어요?
This is room 1209. Could you send someone to carry the luggage?

B 네, 바로 포터를 보내드리겠습니다. 짐은 몇 개나 있습니까?
Yes, I'll send you a porter right away. How many bags do you have?

A 수건을 더 받을 수 있을까요? Can I get more towels?

B 네, 금방 가져다 드리겠습니다. Yes, I'll bring them to you in a minute.

A 피트니스 센터가 있어요? Is there a fitness center?

B 네, 5층에 있습니다. Yeah, it's on the fifth floor.

A 귀중품을 맡길 수 있을까요? Can I leave my valuables with you?

B 네, 물론이죠. 언제 찾아가시겠어요? Yes, of course. When would you like to pick it up?

A 침대 시트가 더러워요. The sheets are dirty.

B 정말 죄송합니다. 새것으로 바꾸어 드리겠습니다.
We're so sorry. We'll change it to a new one.

A 세탁물을 언제 가져다 주시나요? When will you bring any laundry?

B 방 번호가 어떻게 되세요? 잠시만 기다려 주세요.
What's your room number? Please wait a moment.

5 Pronunciation 발음

Track 3-07

☑ Tensification 경음화

When a final consonant 'ㄱ(ㄲ, ㄷ(ㅅ, ㅆ, ㅈ, ㅊ, ㅌ), ㅂ(ㅍ, ㄼ, ㄿ, ㅄ)' is followed by a initial consonant
'ㄱ, ㄷ, ㅂ, ㅅ, ㅈ,' the initial consonant is pronounced as [ㄲ, ㄸ, ㅃ, ㅆ, ㅉ].

Ex 학교 → [학꾜] 목걸이 → [목꺼리] 듣기 → [듣끼] 식당 → [식땅] 학생 → [학쌩]
숙제 → [숙쩨] 옷장 → [옫짱]

In compound nouns, 'ㄱ, ㄷ, ㅂ, ㅅ, ㅈ' following final consonants ㄴ, ㄹ, ㅁ, ㅇ the initial consonant is pronounced as [ㄲ, ㄸ, ㅃ, ㅆ, ㅉ] accordingly.

Ex 눈길 → [눈낄] 물고기 → [물꼬기] 물병 → [물뼝] 비빔밥 → [비빔빱] 봄비 → [봄삐]
일정 → [일쩡]

When ㄱ, ㄷ, ㅅ, ㅈ follows the attributive -(으)ㄹ, the initial consonant is pronounced as [ㄲ, ㄸ, ㅃ, ㅆ, ㅉ] accordingly.

Ex 갈 거예요 → [갈 꺼예요] 청소할게요 → [청소할께요] 할 수 있어요 → [할쑤이써요]
만날 사람 → [만날싸람]

When Chinese syllable ending '-과, 가, 권 in suffix is pronounced as [꽈, 까, 꿘].

Ex 내과 → [내꽈] 치과 → [치꽈] 영양가 → [영양까] 입장권 → [입장꿘] 여권 → [여꿘]

A
- ■ 얼마동안 계실 예정이세요? How long are you planning to stay?
- ⌐ 얼마동안 묵을 예정이세요? How long are you planning to stay?
- ⌐ 얼마동안 머무를 예정이십니까? [How long are you going to stay?]
- ⌐ 며칠 동안 묵으실 거예요? [How many days are you staying?]

B
- 3일 있을 거예요. I'll be three days.
- [3일 묵을 거예요.] [I'll be staying for three days.]
- [3일 동안 묵을 예정이에요.] [I plan to stay for three days.]

A
- ■ 결제는 어떻게 하시겠어요? How would you like to pay?
- ⌐ 어떻게 결제하시겠습니까? How would you like to pay?
- ⌐ 결제 방법은 어떻게 해드릴까요? How would you like to pay?
- ⌐ 결제는 현금으로 하시겠어요? 카드로 하시겠어요?
  Would you like to pay in cash or by a credit card?

B
- 카드로 하겠습니다. I'll pay by a card.
- [신용카드로 계산할게요.] [I'll pay by a credit card.]

A
- ■ 지금 예약을 잡아 드릴까요? Would you like me to make a reservation now?
- ⌐ 지금 예약하시겠어요? Would you like to make a reservation now?
- ⌐ 지금 예약해 드릴까요? Would you like me to make a reservation now?
- ⌐ 어떻게 예약해 드릴까요? How would you like to make a reservation?

7 Culture of Korea

7.1 Anniversaries in Korea 한국의 기념일

The March 1st Independence Movement Day 삼일절 (March 1st)

The March 1st Independence Movement Day is a national holiday commemorating the Independence Movement occurred on March 1, 1919 in Korea.

Children's Day 어린이날 (May 5th)

It is an anniversary established to foster a spirit of love for children and instill dreams and hopes in children so that children, who are the main players of the future society, can grow up to be crystal clear, upright, wise and brave, and it is a legal holiday every year. On this day, commemorative events will be held across the country to respect the character of children and promote happiness. There are many people who spend Children's Day as a family. In particular, the amusement park attracts millions of people. Admission to large parks and zoos is free for children on Children's Day.

Buddha's Birthday 부처님 오신 날 (April 8th of the lunar calendar)

It is the day when Buddha was born and is the largest holiday of the year in Buddhism. Various commemorative events such as memorial service, lantern play, Gwandeung play, Bangsaeng, and Tapdol are held.

The Memorial Day 현충일 (June 6th)

It commemorates all the Koreans who have contributed or died while serving the Republic of Korea. On this day, a memorial ceremony is held in Seoul National Cemetery. At 10 a.m. on Memorial Day, a siren rings all over the country, and people have silent prayers for one minute. The South Korean flag is flown at half-staff.

National Liberation Day of Korea 광복절 (August 15th)

It commemorates the liberation of the Korean Peninsula from the Japanese Empire, and various celebrations are held nationwide, and public institutions and families are also celebrated by hanging the national flag.

The National Foundation Day 개천절 (October 3rd)

Known by the English name National Foundation Day, this holiday celebrates the legendary formation of the first Korean state of Gojoseon in 2333 BC. This date has traditionally been regarded as the date for the founding of the Korean people.

Hangul Day 한글날 (October 9th)

The Korean Alphabet Day, known as Hangeul Day is a national Korean commemorative day marking the invention and proclamation of Hangul (한글), the Korean alphabet, by the 15th century Korean King Sejong the Great.

Christmas 크리스마스 (December 25th)

It is an annual festival commemorating the birth of Jesus Christ as a religious and cultural celebration among billions of people around the world.

7.2 Traditional holiday in Korea 한국의 전통 명절

The Lunar New year 설날

'설날' is a festival and national holiday commemorating the first day of the Chinese lunisolar calendar. It is one of the most important traditional holidays in South Korea. During this time, many Koreans visit family, perform ancestral rites, wear the traditional Korean clothes called '한복', eat rice cake soup called '떡

국', and play folk games. Additionally, children often receive money called '세뱃돈' from their elders after performing a formal bow called '세배'.

Korean Thanksgiving Day 추석

'추석' also known as '한가위' is a major mid-autumn harvest festival and a three-day holiday in South Korea celebrated on the 15th day of the 8th month of the lunar calendar on the full moon. As a celebration of the good harvest, Koreans visit their ancestral hometowns and share a feast of Korean traditional food such as '송편'. There are two major traditions related to '추석': ancestor memorial services at home called '차례' also known as '제사', and family visit to the ancestral graves called '성묘', which is usually accompanied by tidying graves and removing weeds around them.

Dano 단오

'단오' is a Korean traditional holiday that falls on the 5th day of the fifth month of the lunar Korean calendar. South Korea has retained several festivals related to the holiday, one of which is Gangneung Dano Festival designated by UNESCO as a "Intangible Cultural Heritage of Humanity". Traditionally, women washed their hair in water boiled with Sweet Flag called '창포' believed to make one's hair shiny. The persisting folk games of '단오' are the swing called '그네뛰

기' and '씨름. The swing was a game played by women, while '씨름' was a wrestling match among men.

Great Full Moon 대보름

'대보름' is a Korean holiday that celebrates the first full moon of the new year of the lunar Korean calendar which is the Korean version of the First Full Moon Festival. This holiday is accompanied by many traditions. People crack nuts with their teeth, believing that this will keep one's teeth healthy for the year. In the countryside, people climb mountains, braving cold weather, trying to catch the first rise of the moon. It is said that the first person to see the moon rise will

have good luck all year or a wish will be granted. The traditional foods of '대보름' have a lot of connections with superstition.

(1) 여행을 갈까요, 가요.　　(2) 책을 읽을까요, 읽어요.
(3) 밥을 먹을까요, 먹어요.　　(4) 노래를 부를까요, 불러요.

(1) 선물을 받고 싶어요.　　(2) 휴대폰을 사고 싶어요.
(3) 쇼핑을 하고 싶어요.　　(4) 한국어를 잘 하고 싶어요.

(1) 책을 찾아 주세요.　　(2) 조용히 해 주세요.
(3) 문법을 가르쳐 주세요.　　(4) 문을 열어 주세요.

(1) 좀 더 기다려 주시겠어요?　　(2) 내일 아침에 전화해 주시겠어요?
(3) 천천히 말씀해 주시겠어요?　　(4) 이것 좀 치워 주시겠어요?

(1) 김치는 맵지만 맛있어요.
(2) 휴대 전화가 예쁘지만 비싸요.
(3) 한국어 공부는 어렵지만 재미있어요.
(4) 겨울은 춥지만 여름은 더워요.

(1) 비빔밥이 맛있어요.　　(2) 자동차가 많아요.
(3) 지하철이 빨라요.　　(4) 제임스씨가 밥을 먹어요.

(1) 택시로 갈 거예요.　　(2) 현금으로 지불하겠어요.
(3) 젓가락으로 먹어요.　　(4) 유트브로 공부해요.

(1) 아침에 운동을 하겠습니다.　　(2) 저는 비빔밥을 먹겠습니다.
(3) 제가 커피를 사 오겠습니다.　　(4) 예약을 확인해 드리겠습니다.

(1) 팔십삼   (2) 칠백사십구   (3) 삼천백구십오   (4) 사천칠백

(5) 육십   (6) 오백이십구만백

(1) 오후 세시 이십사분   (2) 오전 일곱시 삼십육분

(3) 오전 열두시 삼십분   (4) 오후 한시 오십오분

(1) 안 더워요, 덥지 않아요.   (2) 운전 안 했어요, 운전하지 않았어요.

(3) 안 비싸요, 비싸지 않아요.   (4) 안 어려워요, 어렵지 않아요.

메모

4

지금 주문하시겠습니까?

May I take your order now?

Unit 4

지금 주문하시겠습니까?
May I take your order now?

---

1 **Study Objectives** 학습 목표

✎ To guide and take an order in a restaurant (식당 안내와 주문)
✎ To introduce Korean food and how to eat them (한국 음식 소개)
✎ To receive orders and reserve meals (주문받기와 식사 예약)
✎ To learn room service and eating etiquette (룸 서비스와 식사 예절)

2 **Vocabulary** 어휘

2.1 **Dialogue Vocabulary** 본문 어휘

Noun 명사 ✎

레스토랑 restaurant	메뉴판 the menu	치킨바비큐 chicken BBQ
샐러드 salad	토스트 toast	감자튀김 fried potato
음료수 beverage	계절 음료 seasonal drink	인기 popularity
호실 room number	파스타 pasta	필라프 pilaf
제철 in season	야채 vegetable	과일 fruit
접시 dish / plate	크림 cream	설탕 sugar
포크 fork	룸서비스 room service	
이탈리안 드레싱 Italian dressing		

Verb 동사 🖊

빼다 remove   주문하다 order   나오다 come out

Others 나머지 🖊

따뜻하다 warm   추가 additional   많다 a lot / much
먼저 first   빨리 quickly   함께 together

2.2 Related Vocabulary 관련 어휘

음식과 음료수 Food & Beverage 🖊

햄버거 hamburger   치즈버거 cheese burger   김밥 gimbap
감자튀김 French fries   냉면 naengmyeon   떡볶이 tteokbokki
김치찌개 kimchi stew   비빔밥 bibimbap   불고기 bulgogi
설렁탕 seolleongtang   라면 ramen   김치 kimchi
빵 bread   에그 egg   통밀 whole wheat
토스트 toast   베이컨 bacon   우유 milk
주스 juice   커피 coffee   맥주 beer
물 water   홍차 black tea   녹차 green tea
사이다 soda pop   콜라 cola

과일과 야채 Fruits and Vegetables 🖊

사과 apple   배 pear   오렌지 orange
바나나 banana   파인애플 pineapple   망고 mango
파파야 papaya   용과 dragon fruit   수박 watermelon
포도 grape   토마토 tomato   딸기 strawberry
배추 Chinese cabbage   당근 carrot   감자 potato
오이 cucumber

맛 표현 Expressions of Flavor

달다 to be sweet　　　　맵다 to be spicy　　　　짜다 to be salty

시다 to be sour　　　　쓰다 to be bitter　　　　맛있다 to be yummy

매콤하다 to be slightly spicy　　칼칼하다 to bevery spicy　　얼큰하다 to be quite spicy

아리다 to beunpleasantly spicy　짭짤하다 to bepleasantly salty　새콤하다 to be slightly sour

시디시다 to be very sour　　쌉쌀하다 to be slightly bitter　쓰디쓰다 to be very bitter

개운하다 to be refreshing　　느끼하다 to be greasy　　떫다 to be bitter & sour

비리다 to be fishy　　　부드럽다 to be soft　　　싱겁다 (밍밍하다) to be bland

맛없다 to be gross　　　달콤하다 to be slightly sweet　상큼하다 to be refreshing

쫄깃쫄깃하다 to be chewy

감미롭다 to be sweet and tasty　　　달달하다 to have sweet undertones

달짝지근하다 to have a touch of sweetness　짭짜름하다 to have a touch of saltiness

시큼하다 to be unpleasantly very sour　　삼삼하다 to be tasty and slightly salty

새콤달콤하다 to be sweet and sour　　　살살 녹다 (verb) to melts in one's mouth

얼얼하다 to be very spicy (lasts for a long time)　구수하다 to be hearty (stronger than 고소하다)

감칠맛이 나다 to be tasty (usually describes a savory dish)

고소하다 to be savory (usually describes grainy or nutty flavors)

담백하다 to be very light (the opposite of 느끼하다)

시원하다 to be refreshing (used more than 개운하다)

음식 소개와 주문 Introduction and Ordering of Food

손님 guest / customer　　다이어트 diet　　　달러 dollar

센트 cent　　　　　룸서비스 room service　찌다 steam

튀기다 fry　　　　　굽다 broil　　　　데우다 heat

끓이다 boil　　　　볶다 roast　　　　가져가다 take it with you

시키다 order　　　　저기요 Excuse me　　다음 next

더블	double		지금	right now		필요한	necessary
추가로	in addition		더	more			

3 Dialogue 대화

Track 4-01

Dialogue 1 **Receiving Orders 1_Restaurant** 주문 받기 1_레스토랑

A 저기요~ 여기 메뉴판 좀 주세요. Excuse me~ Can I see the menu?

B 네~ 여기 있습니다. Okay. Here it is.
    지금 주문하시겠습니까? May I take your order now?

A 네, 치킨 바비큐하고 베이컨 토스트 1개 주세요. 맥주도 2병 주세요.
    Yes, could I have a chicken barbecue and a bacon toast. Two bottles of beer too, please.

B 네, 알겠습니다. 샐러드를 추가하시겠어요? Yes, sir. Would you like to add a salad?

Counting Units 단위명사 ▶

Korean counting units are essential in using numbers in everyday life and are used to help us count different items. There are various counting units to count objects in Korean. For example, '개' is most commonly used to count general inanimate items. '병', '잔', and '그릇' are used for bottles, cups or glasses, and bowls, respectively.

When numbers and counting units are used together, the counting units take the forms '한, 두, 세, 네, 열한, 열두, 열세, 열네, and 스무' rather than '하나(1), 둘(2), 셋(3), 넷(4), 열하나 (11), 열둘(12), 열셋(13), 열넷(14), and 스물(20)'. When using counting units with the native Korean numbers system, the order is to use the object or item + number + counting units. Note that there is a space between the words.

오렌지 한 개 주세요. Give me an orange, please.

맥주 두 병 주세요. Give me two bottles of beer, please.

커피 세 잔 주세요. Give me three cups of coffee, please.

냉면 네 그릇 주세요. Give me four bowls of Naengmyeon, please.

A list of the most common Korean counting unit is as follows:

Counting Unit	Meaning	Counting Unit	Meaning	Counting Unit	Meaning
개	items	명	people	분	people(honorific)
병	bottles	잔(컵)	glasses, cups	그릇	bowl, dish, plate
조각	slices	권	books notebooks	마리	animals
살	age	대	cars machines	자루	sack long objects

알	small & round objects	장	pieces of paper	벌	clothes
켤레	pairs of shoes	그루	trees	채	houses buildings
척	ships	판	whole piece game	덩이	lump chunk
상자	boxes	공기	bowl	접시	dish, plate
바구니	basket	통	bucket, pail, tub	포기	grass or trees by the root
송이	bunch, cluster	단	bundle, sheaf	세트	sets of sofas
쌍	sets of two	가지	kinds, varieties	군데	places
번	times	층	floors in a building	시간	duration in hours
주일	weeks	달	duration in months		

♣ Complete the following dialogues as in the example.

Ex A: 모자가 몇 개 있어요?   B: 세 개 있어요. (3)

(1) A: 책이 몇 _____ 있어요?   B: _____. (2)

(2) A: 맥주가 몇 _____ 있어요?   B: _____. (1)

(3) A: 강아지가 몇 _____ 있어요?   B: _____. (5)

(4) A: 장미꽃이 몇 _____ 있어요?   B: _____. (4)

–주세요

Adding '주세요' after N and at the end of the sentence means that the speaker requests N (noun) from the listener. This pattern is commonly used in a restaurant or a market when ordering food or buying something. You add 을/를 after the noun, however, this is often taken out in conversation.

N주세요
닭갈비 + 주세요 → 닭갈비 주세요.
삼겹살 + 주세요 → 삼겹살 주세요.

A: 어서 오세요. 뭐 드릴까요? Welcome. What would you like to have?

B: 불고기하고 김치찌개 주세요. Bulgogi and kimchi stew, please.

A: 커피하고 녹차 있습니다. 무엇으로 드릴까요?

   We have coffee and green tea. What would you like?

B: 아메리카노 한 잔 주세요. I'd like a cup of Americano, please.

A: 오렌지, 배, 수박이 있어요. 뭐 드릴까요?

   There are oranges, pears, and watermelons. What do you want?

B: 그럼, 수박 주세요. Then, watermelon, please.

🍀 **Order the following food at a restaurant as in the example.**

Ex 삼겹살 → 삼겹살 주세요.

(1) 불고기 → _____.

(2) 물냉면 → _____.

(3) 비빔밥 → _____.

(4) 삼계탕 → _____.

–하고

'하고' is inserted to connect two nouns (N and N') which corresponds to 'and' in English.

N하고
커피 + 하고 + 샌드위치 → 커피하고 샌드위치
김치 + 하고 + 물 → 김치하고 물

커피하고 샌드위치(를) 주세요. Please give me coffee and sandwich.

김치하고 물(을) 주세요. Please give me kimchi and water.

비빔밥 하나하고 냉면 둘 주세요. One bibimbap and two naengmyeon, please.

☞ Usage of '하고' :

불고기 + 하고 + 갈비 + 하고 + 김치 → 불고기하고 갈비하고 김치 bulgogi, galbi and kimchi

🍀 **Connect two nouns using '하고' as in the example.**

Ex <u>콜라 한 병하고 맥주 두 병</u> 주세요.   (콜라 1, 맥주 2)

(1) _____ 주세요.   (커피 3, 녹차 4)

(2) _____ 주세요.   (소주 2, 맥주 1)

(3) _____ 주세요.　　(피자 1, 오렌지 주스 1)

(4) _____ 주세요.　　(냉면 5, 콜라 3)

Dialogue 2　**Receiving Orders 2_Fast Food Restaurant** 주문 받기 2_패스트푸드점

A　다음 손님이요. 뭘 드릴까요?　Next customer, please. What can I get for you?

B　더블 치즈버거 하나 주세요.　I'd like a double cheeseburger, please.

A　네, 알겠습니다.　Yes, I see.

　　여기에서 드실 거예요? 가져가실 거예요?　Is this for here, or to go?

B　여기서 먹을 거예요.　Here, please.

　　그리고 감자튀김도 함께 주세요.　And, I'd like fries, please.

A　음료수는 뭘로 드시겠어요?　What would you like to drink?

B　계절 음료가 있어요?　Do you have seasonal drinks?

A　네, 피치레몬 블랜디드나 딸기요거트 블랜디드는 어떠세요?

　　Yes, how about peach lemon blended or strawberry yogurt blended?

　　요즘 인기가 많아요.　It's very popular these days.

B 그럼 피치레몬 블랜디드로 주세요. Then I'll have a peach lemon blended.

네, 모두 250바트입니다. Yes, it's 250 baht in all.

Key Grammar 핵심 문법

-(으)ㄹ 거예요 ▶

'-(으)ㄹ 거예요' is used to express a future plan or intention and means the same as 'will' or 'going to' in English.

Verb stem ending with a vowel or ㄹ → -ㄹ 거예요	Verb stem ends with consonant → -을 거예요
하다: 하 + -ㄹ 거예요 → 할 거예요 팔다: 파 + -ㄹ 거예요 → 팔 거예요	읽다: 읽 + -을 거예요 → 읽을 거예요 씻다: 씻 + -을 거예요 → 씻을 거예요

내일 뭐 할 거예요? What are you going to do tomorrow?

뭘 팔 거예요? What are you going to sell?

나는 오늘 오후 도서관에서 책을 읽을 거예요. I'm going to read a book in the library this afternoon.

🍀 **Complete the sentence using '-(으)ㄹ 거예요' as in the example.**

Ex 내일 / 책 / 읽다 → <u>내일 책을 읽을 거예요.</u>

(1) 이번 주말 / 친구 / 만나다 → _____.

(2) 내년 / 한국 / 여행하다 → _____.

(3) 오늘 저녁 / 텔레비전 / 보다 → _____.

(4) 다음 주 토요일 / 사진 / 찍다 → _____.

-(이)나

'(이)나' attaches after the noun indicating that it hasn't been decided which noun/object will be acted on. It corresponds to 'or' in English.

Nouns ending with a vowel → 나	Nouns ending with a consonant → 이나
오렌지 + -나 → 오렌지나	옷 + -이나 → 옷이나

저는 오렌지나 사과를 먹고 싶어요. I want to eat an orange or an apple.

저는 오늘 김치찌개나 갈비를 먹을 거예요. I'll eat Kimchi stew or galbi today.

배가 고프면 빵이나 과자를 드세요. If you're hungry, please eat bread or snacks.

🍀 **Fill in the blank using** '이나' **or** '나' **as in the example.**

> Ex   A: 몇 시에 갈까요?   B: 3시나 4시에 오세요.

(1) A: 뭐 마시겠어요?   B: 소주_____ 맥주 주세요.

(2) A: 저녁에 뭘 드세요?   B: 비빔밥_____ 김치찌개 먹어요.

(3) A: 공항에 어떻게 가세요?   B: 버스_____ 택시를 타요.

(4) A: 내일 어디에 가요?   B: 미술관_____ 박물관에 가요.

은/는 어떠세요?

'은/는 어떠세요?' attaches after the noun and is usually used when we ask other person's opinion or feeling.

Nouns ending with a vowel → 는 어떠세요	Nouns ending with a consonant → 은 어떠세요
커피 + 는 어떠세요? → 커피는 어떠세요?	골프장 + 은 어떠세요? → 골프장은 어떠세요?

저 골프장은 어떠세요? How about that golf course?

주말에 테니스나 수영은 어떠세요? How about tennis or swimming on the weekend?

선물로 화장품이나 커피는 어떠세요? How about cosmetics or coffee as a present?

점심에 샌드위치나 피자는 어떠세요? How about a sandwich or pizza for lunch?

🍀 **Create the sentences using** '–은/는 어떠세요?' **as in the example.**

Ex (이, 옷) → 이 옷은 어떠세요?

(1) (요즘, 건강) → _____

(2) (오늘, 기분) → _____

(3) (오늘 저녁, 모임) → _____

(4) (내일, 출발) → _____

Track 4-03

A 안녕하세요. 룸서비스입니다. Hello, this is room service.

B 룸 서비스를 주문하고 싶은데요. 235호실이에요.
Yes, I'd like to order room service. I'm in Room 235.

A 알겠습니다. 손님, 뭘 드시겠습니까?
All right, sir. What would you like to eat?

B 쉬림프 필라프하고 토마토 파스타 1인분 그리고 과일 한 접시요
Shrimp pilaf, 1 serving of tomato pasta and a plate of fruit, please.

파스타가 많이 매워요? Is the pasta very spicy?

A 많이 맵지 않아요. 제철 야채가 함께 나옵니다.
It's not that spicy. It comes with seasonal vegetables.

음료는 어떻게 하시겠어요? What would you like for the drink?

B 따뜻한 커피를 두 잔 주세요 Two cups of hot coffee, please.

크림은 빼 주세요 Please take out the cream.

설탕만 주세요. Just sugar, please.

A 알겠습니다. 추가로 더 시킬 것이 있으세요?
Okay. Do you have anything else to order?

B 이탈리안 드레싱을 갖다 주시겠어요? Could you bring me some Italian dressing?

포크도 하나만 더 주세요. One more fork, please.

A 물론이죠. 가져다 드리겠습니다 Sure. I'll get it for you.

B 네, 좀 빨리 부탁드려요. Yes, please hurry up.

Key Grammar 핵심 문법

을/를

'을/를' indicates that the noun preceding it is the object of the sentence.

Nouns ending with a vowel → 를	Nouns ending with a consonant → 을
김치 + 를 → 김치를	비빔밥 + 을 → 비빔밥을

저는 바나나를 먹어요. I eat a banana.

저는 한국어 책을 읽어요. I read a Korean book.

내 친구는 김치를 좋아해요. My friend likes kimchi.

🍀 **Complete the following sentences as in the example.**

Ex 푸엉 씨 / 한국어 책 / 읽다 → 푸엉 씨가 한국어 책을 읽어요.

(1) 수안 씨 / 빵 / 먹다 → _____.

(2) 우리 / 한국어 / 공부하다 → _____.

(3) 민수 씨 / 음악 / 듣다 → _____.

(4) 리타 / 방 / 청소하다 → _____.

–(으)ㄴ데요

'–(으)ㄴ데요' gives a sentence the feeling of disagreement, expectation, or surprise. As such, it corresponds to 'Well, in my case', '… and?' or '… but?' or '(I'm surprised to learn that)… is so…' in English. It is also used to set background information for natural conversation.

Adjective stem ending with a vowel or ㄹ or '이다', '아니다' → –ㄴ데요	Adjective stem ends with consonant → –은데요
예쁘다: 예쁘 + –ㄴ데요 → 예쁜데요 멀다: 멀 + –ㄴ데요 → 먼데요 ('ㄹ' is dropped)	많다: 많 + –은데요 → 많은데요 좋다: 좋 + –은데요 → 좋은데요

여자 친구가 정말 예쁜데요. Your girlfriend is really pretty.

여기에서 공항은 아주 먼데요. The airport is very far from here.

백화점에 사람들이 많은데요. There are a lot of people in the department store.

–있다, –없다 → –는데요	For Verbs → –는데요
재미있다: 재미있 + 는데요 → 재미있는데요 맛없다: 맛없 + 는데요 → 맛없는데요	잘하다: 잘하 + –는데요 → 잘하는데요 먹었다 : 먹었 + –는데요 → 먹었는데요

이 컴퓨터 게임은 정말 재미있는데요. This computer game is really fun.

이 김치는 별로 맛없는데요. This kimchi isn't that good.

한국말을 아주 잘하는데요. You speak Korean really well.

저는 벌써 저녁을 먹었는데요. I've already had dinner.

♣ Fill in the blanks using '-(으)ㄴ/는데요' as in the example.

> Ex A: 저 가수 좀 보세요.　　　　　B: 와~, 정말 <u>대단한데요.</u> (대단하다)

(1) A: 우리 같이 밥 먹으러 갈까요?

　 B: 미안해요. 좀 _____. (바쁘다)

(2) A: 찰리 씨, 이 컴퓨터 좀 고쳐주세요.

　 B: 글쎄요. _____. (잘 모르겠다)

(3) A: 몇 분이세요?

　 B: _____. (세 명이다)

(4) A: 우리 같이 산책하러 가요.

　 B: 미안해요. _____. (시간이 없다)

–만

▼

'만' is attached to a noun when limiting the field to one thing, excluding all the others. It is also used to limit the number or quantity to the minimum state.

N만
물 한 잔 + 만 → 물 한 잔만 삼십 분 + 만 → 삼십 분만

물 한 잔만 주세요. I'd like a glass of water, please.

사과 한 개만 더 주세요. One more apple, please.

호텔 방에 저만 있어요. I'm the only one in the hotel room.

❦ **Complete the following sentences as in the example.**

> **Ex** 동생 / 컴퓨터 게임 / 하다 → <u>동생은 컴퓨터 게임만 해요.</u>

(1) 저 / 한국말 / 하다 → _____.

(2) 민수 씨 / 고기 / 좋아하다 → _____.

(3) 제임스 씨 / 신용카드 / 있다 → _____.

(4) 내 친구 / 한국 음식 / 먹다 → _____.

4 Response Exercise 응답 연습

Guiding 안내하기

Track 4-04

A 안녕하세요? '김수진'으로 예약했습니다. Hello, I made a reservation for Kim Soo-jin.

B 어서오세요. 이쪽으로 오세요. Welcome. This way, please.

[네, 이쪽으로 모시겠습니다.] [Yes, this way, please.]

[어서오세요. 테이블 안내를 도와드리겠습니다.]
[Welcome. Let me guide you to the table.]

[네, 잠시만요. 예약 확인해 드리겠습니다.]
[Yes, hold on. Let me confirm your reservation.]

A 예약은 안 했어요. 혹시 두 사람 자리가 있어요?
I didn't make a reservation. Do you happen to have a table for two?

B 네, 기다리시면 자리를 안내해 드리겠습니다. Yes, please wait to be seated.

A 누가 더 오실 건가요? Who else is coming?

B 네, 1명이 더 올 거예요. Yes, we're expecting one more person.

To take an order 주문 받기

Track 4-05

A 여기 메뉴판이 있습니다. 메뉴를 정하시면 불러 주세요.
Here's the menu. Please call me when you decide on the menu.

[여기, 메뉴가 있습니다.] [Here is the menu.]

[저희 특별 메뉴를 (오늘 코스 요리를) 추천해 드릴까요?]
[Shall we recommend our special menu (today's course meal)?]

B 네, 감사합니다. Please, thank you.

A 드시고 가실 거예요? Is this for here?

B 아니요, 포장해 주세요. No, to go, please.

[아니요, 가져갈 거예요.] [No, I'll take it to go.]

A 메뉴판이 있습니다. 천천히 보세요. 다시 올게요.
Here's the menu. Take your time. I'll be back.

B 네, 잠시 시간을 주세요. Yes, give us a second please.

A 어떤 걸로 드시겠습니까? What would you like to have?

B 이걸로 할게요. I'll take this one.

A 여기요, 링기니 파스타 하나 주세요. Excuse me, can I have one Ringini pasta, please?

B 정말 죄송합니다. 지금 링기니 파스타는 안 되는데요. 펜네 파스타는 어떠세요?
I'm so sorry. We can't make Ringini pasta right now. How about Penne pasta?

[죄송합니다. 오늘 추천 메뉴를 안내해 드릴까요?]
[I'm sorry. Shall I introduce you to today's recommended menu?]

To confirm one's request 요청 확인하기

Track 4-06

A 여기요, 김치 좀 더 주세요. Excuse me, please give me some more kimchi.

B 네, 알겠습니다. 바로 드리겠습니다. Yes, I got it. I'll give it to you right away.

[네, 여기 있습니다.] Yes, here it is.

[물론이죠, 바로 드릴게요.] Sure, I'll give it to you right away.

[여기요. 맛있게 드세요.] Here. Please enjoy your meal.

A 고기가 덜 익었어요. The meat is undercooked.

[고기가 너무 익었어요.] [The meat is overcooked.]

B 다시 만들어 드리겠습니다. We'll make it again.

A 미안하지만 다른 자리로 옮길 수 있을까요? I'm sorry, but can I move to another seat?

B 네, 그럼 저쪽 테이블로 옮겨 드리겠습니다.
Yes, then I'll move you to the table over there.

To get a reservation 예약 받기

Track 4-07

A 토요일 저녁식사를 예약하고 싶어요.
I'd like to make a reservation for dinner on Saturday.

6시로 예약해 주세요. Please make a reservation for 6 o'clock.

B 네, 됩니다. 몇 분이세요? Yes, you can. How many people are there in your party?

[네, 좋습니다. 금연석으로 해 드릴까요?]

Okay, good. Would you like a non-smoking seat?

[죄송하지만 자리가 다 찼습니다.] I'm sorry, but all seats are taken.

A 오늘 저녁에 자리를 예약하고 싶습니다.
I'd like to reserve a table for this evening.

B 몇 시에 오실 건가요? What time will you come?

[언제 도착하실 건가요?] [When will you arrive?]

To confirm the order details 주문 내용 확인하기

Track 4-08

A 다 주문하신 건가요? Have you ordered everything?

B 네, 이걸로 주세요. Okay, I'll take this one.

A 더 필요한 거 없으세요? Do you need anything else?

B 네, 지금은 그걸로 됐어요. Okay, that's all for now.

A 손님, 주문 도와드릴까요? May I help you with your order?

B 네, 삼겹살 2인분 주세요. Yes, two servings of pork belly, please.

[네, 스테이크와 파스타 주세요.] [Yes, steak and pasta, please.]

[네, 커피 2잔하고 맥주 1병 주세요.]

[Yes, 2 cups of coffee and 1 bottle of beer, please.]

[네, 햄버거 두 개 포장해 주세요.] [Yes, can I get two hamburgers to go?]

5　Pronunciation 발음

✓ Nasalization (비음화)

Track 4-09

If the final consonant is [ㄱ, ㄷ, ㅂ], it is pronounced as [ㅇ, ㄴ, ㅁ] respectively when followed by the initial consonant ㄴ, ㅁ. In this case when the consonant ㄴ or ㅁ comes after the syllable ending in ㅂ, we pronounce ㅂ as [ㅁ].

Ex　갑니다 → [감니다]　합니까 → [함니까]　십만원 → [심마눤]　이십 명 → [이심 명]

When the final ㅁ or ㅇ is fronted by the consonant ㄹ, we pronounce this ㄹ as [ㄴ].

Ex　음료수 → [음뇨수]　정리 → [정니]　정류장 → [정뉴장]　종로 → [종노]

6　Additional Expression 추가 표현

A	■ 주문하시겠습니까?　May I take your order?
	┚ 주문하시겠어요?　Would you like to order?
	┚ 주문 도와드릴까요?　May I help you with your order?
	┚ 뭐 드릴까요?　What would you like to have?
B	메뉴판 좀 보여주세요.　Please show me the menu.
	음, 여기 뭐가 맛있어요?　Um, what's good here?

A	■ 더 시킬 것이 있으세요?　Do you have anything else to order?
	┚ 더 필요한 거 있으세요?　Do you need anything else?
B	네, 더 추가할 것이 있어요.　Yes, I have more to add.
	아니요, 괜찮습니다.　No, it's okay.

A	■ 음료수는 뭘로 드시겠어요?	What would you like to drink?
	┛음료수는 뭘로 드릴까요?	What would you like to drink?
	┛음료수는 뭘로 하시겠어요?	What would you like to drink?

7 Culture of Korea

7.1 Typical dining set in Korea 전형적인 한식탁

In Korea, side dishes are usually served with the main dish, so you don't have to order them separately. Water is usually also provided free of charge.

Characteristics of broth based Korean foods 국/탕/찌개/전골의 특징

"Guk"(국), "Tang"(탕), "Jjigae"(찌개) and "Jeongol"(전골) all have something in common that they are foods with broth(국물), but there is a difference in the amount of broth and the way they are boiled. "Guk" means a food boiled by pouring a lot of water into meat, fish, and vegetables and seasoning them. "Tang" refers to a soup with a lot of ingredients and less broth, which is also used as an honorific term for "guk." These two have differences in their use as everyday food ('Guk') and ritual food ('Tang"). "Jjigae" means a side dish boiled with various spices by catching broth in an earthen pot or small pot and putting meat, vegetables, and tofu, and soy sauce, soybean paste, red pepper paste, and salted fish soup. "Jeongol" is a food that is boiled by mixing seasoning, vegetables, mushrooms, and seafood with chopped meat, putting them in a hot pot frame, and pouring a little water. "Jjigae" and "Jeongol" are foods that boil less soup than "Guk" and the use of earthen pot or hot pot frames is compared to "Guk" or "Tang" previously mentioned.

7.2 10 Basic Rules of Korean Dining Etiquette
한국인의 식사예절 10가지 기본원칙

1. Say '잘 먹겠습니다.'

Say '잘 먹겠습니다', which means 'I will eat well.', or 'I will enjoy this meal.' – a polite way of appreciation for the food you receive and the person who cooked it. It's akin to saying grace before eating, 'Thank you for the food'.

2. Elder first

Like most Asians, respect for elders is a core value in Korean culture that is also practised at the dining table. Typically, the elder picks up his/her chopsticks first to start off the family meal. If you happened to be the eldest? Well, don't keep everyone waiting!

3. Start with soup

Begin your meal with a taste of soup or stews. This warms your tongue and preps your taste-buds for the flavorful dishes to come.

4. Bowl, chopsticks and spoon

Chopsticks are for dishes, a spoon is for rice and soup. Don't hold your chopsticks and spoon together at the same time, never use your chopsticks like skewers, and never stab them in your bowl of rice – which is a funeral ritual. A Korean meal typically has an array of shared dishes, so don't poke or dig around them with your chopsticks, pick what you want, and enjoy it from your personal dish plate. Keep your rice bowl on the table at all times while eating.

5. Don't hoard

Sharing is caring, cliché as that may be, but absolutely true in a Korean meal. So, make sure everyone can enjoy the shared dishes. Always take just enough from each time, and don't hoard a pile of food on your personal plate and bowl.

6. Balance your flavors

Korean meals have many tastes and flavors from the combination of soup/stew, rice, meat and veggie dishes. Temper the spiciness with rice and soup, and balance the heat of meat with cooling veggies. Basically, enjoy every dish at the table. Being choosy means missing out.

7. Eat calmly, chew thoroughly

Unlike some cultures where slurping is actually a sign of loving the food, Koreans prefer quiet enjoyment. So, sip your soup or stew slowly to savor every taste. Don't wolf down your food, or chomp with your mouth open; but chew and appreciate the warmth, excitement and umami flavrs in every mouthful.

8. Stay focused

Enjoying your food and company is more important than scrolling your phone. So, don't. No TV, magazine or newspaper either, please. Focus on your meal and conversations with your loved ones at the table.

9. Pass with both hands, pour for others

When passing bowls, glasses, or dishes, always use both hands to show respect. For Koreans, it's also considered rude to refill your drink, especially for alcohol. Always pour for others at the table, and let them fill yours.

10. Finish with grace

After you filled your tummy and satiated your taste-buds, finish by placing your chopsticks and spoon beside your bowl or plate, not atop. Also, make sure there are no leftovers. And finally, say '잘 먹었습니다', which means 'I ate well', to show your love and appreciation.

Answers

(1) 권, 두 권 있어요.

(2) 병, 한 병 있어요.

(3) 마리, 다섯 마리 있어요.

(4) 송이, 네 송이 있어요.

(1) 불고기 주세요.

(2) 물냉면 주세요.

(3) 비빔밥 주세요.

(4) 삼계탕 주세요.

(1) 커피 세 잔하고 녹차 네 잔 주세요.

(2) 소주 두 병하고 맥주 한 병 주세요.

(3) 피자 한 조각하고 오렌지 주스 한 잔 주세요.

(4) 냉면 오 인분하고 콜라 세 병 주세요.

Answers
Dialogue 2

(1) 이번 주말에 친구를 만날 거예요.

(2) 내년에 한국을 여행할 거예요.

(3) 오늘 저녁에 텔레비전을 볼 거예요.

(4) 다음 주 토요일에 사진을 찍을 거예요.

(1) 나 (2) 이나 (3) 나 (4) 이나

(1) 요즘 건강은 어떠세요?

(2) 오늘 기분이 어떠세요?

(3) 오늘 저녁 모임은 어떠세요?

(4) 내일 출발은 어떠세요?

(1) 수안 씨가 빵을 먹어요.   (2) 우리는 한국어를 공부해요.

(3) 민수 씨가 음악을 들어요.   (4) 리타가 방을 청소해요.

(1) 바쁜데요.   (2) 잘 모르겠는데요.

(3) 세 명인데요.   (4) 시간이 없는데요.

(1) 저는 한국말만 해요.   (2) 민수 씨는 고기만 좋아해요.

(3) 제임스 씨는 신용카드만 있어요.   (4) 내 친구는 한국 음식만 먹어요.

메모

5

편의점은 약국 옆에 있습니다
The convenience store is next to the pharmacy

Unit 5

편의점은 약국 옆에 있습니다

The convenience store is next to the pharmacy

1 Study Objectives 학습 목표

✎ To know expressions to providing locations and places (장소와 위치)

✎ To know expressions to providing directions and finding a way (방향과 길 찾기)

✎ To learn expressions about means of transportation and car rental service
(교통 수단과 렌터카 대여)

2 Vocabulary 어휘

2.1 Dialogue Vocabulary 본문 어휘

Noun 명사

근처 near	편의점 convenience store	왼쪽 the left
약국 pharmacy	옆 next to	관광객 tourist
택시 taxi	방법 method	건너편 the opposite side
버스 bus	정류장 stop /station	렌터카 rental car
종류 kind	작년 last year	보험 insurance
국제면허증 international license		시간 time

Verb 동사 🖍️

타다 get on | 내리다 get off | 걸리다 take (time)
보이다 be seen / appear | 빌리다 borrow | 운전하다 drive
준비하다 prepare

Others 기타 🖍️

많다 many /much | 얼마나 How much | 멀다 far
혹시 by any chance | 쯤 about

2.2 Related Vocabulary 관련 어휘

장소 Places 🖍️

박물관 museum	미술관 art museum	백화점 department store
극장(영화관) theater	공원 park	호텔 hotel
미용실 hair salon	교회 church	노래방 karaoke room
소방서 fire station	세탁소 laundry	도서관 library
문구점 stationery store	병원 hospital	꽃집 flower shop
집 house	은행 bank	경찰서 police station
커피숍 coffee shop	식당 restaurant	기차역 train station
화장실 washroom	버스 정류장 bus stop	시장 market
응급실 emergency room	놀이 공원 amusement park	공항 airport
학교 school	쇼핑 센터 shopping center	가게 store
기숙사 dormitory	대사관 embassy	우체국 post office
환전소 currency exchange	카페 café	
관광안내소 tourist information center		

위치와 방향 Locations and Directions

위 above	아래 below	오른쪽 the right
사이 between	안 inside	밖 outside
앞 front	뒤 back	저기 there
똑바로 straight		

교통수단과 길찾기 Means of Transportation and Finding a Way

기차 train	지하철 subway	비행기 air plane
오토바이 motorcycle	자전거 bicycle	배 ship
트라이시클 tricycle	연비 fuel efficiency	소형차 compact car
승용차 sedan	컨버터블 convertible car	차 car
층 floor	가깝다 near	갈아타다 transfer

---

3   **Dialogue** 대화

Track 5-01

> **Dialogue 1**   **Location and Direction** 위치와 방향

A 저, 이 근처에 편의점이 있어요? Excuse me, is there a convenience store nearby?

B 네, 있습니다. Yes, there is.

A 어디에 있어요? Where is it?

B 나가셔서 왼쪽으로 가세요. Go out and turn left.
편의점은 약국 옆에 있습니다. The convenience store is next to the pharmacy

---

Key Grammar 핵심 문법

-에

'에' is attached to a place noun and mainly used with the verbs 가다, 오다, 도착하다 and 돌아가다 to indicate the direction. It corresponds to 'to' in English.

-에
식당 + 에 → 식당에
공항 + 에 → 공항에

....

저는 식당에 가요. I go to the restaurant.

친구가 공항에 도착해요. My friend arrives at the airport.

수민 씨가 회사에 다녀요. Soomin works at a company.

☞ '에' is also added to 있다/없다 to express the location of a person or thing. It corresponds to 'in', 'at' or 'on' in English.

....

호텔에 수영장이 없어요. There is no swimming pool in the hotel.

은행 뒤에 시장이 있어요. There's a department store behind the bank.

저는 주말에 보통 집에 있어요. I usually stay home on the weekends.

♣ Complete the following dialogues as in the example.

> **Ex** A: 제임스 씨, 편의점이 어디에 있어요?
>
> B: <u>커피숍 옆에 있어요.</u> (커피숍 옆)

(1) A: 민수 씨, 환전소가 어디에 있어요?

　　B: _____. (백화점 앞)

(2) A: 안나 씨, 화장실이 어디에 있어요?

　　B: _____. (커피숍 안)

(3) A: 히엔 씨, ABC 호텔이 어디에 있어요?

　　B: _____. (경찰서 뒤)

(4) A: 푸엉 씨, 세탁소가 어디에 있어요?

　　B: _____. (만나 식당 건너편)

–아/어/여서 (Sequence) [1]

'아/어/여서' is attached to a verb, and is used to present incidents chronologically. As the front sentence becomes the condition of the back sentence, it is used to indicate a temporal sequence.

'–아서' is attached to stems ending in the vowels ㅏ or ㅗ.	'–어서' is attached to stems ending in other vowels.	'–해서' is attached to stems ending in –하다.
만나다: 만나 + 아서 → 만나서 오다: 오 + 아서 → 와서	만들다: 만들 + 어서 → 만들어서 쓰다: 쓰 + 어서 → 써서 (* 'ㅡ' is dropped from the verb stem)	공부하다: 공부 + 해서 → 공부해서 운동하다: 운동 + 해서 → 운동해서

여기 앉아서 차 한잔 마셔요.   Let's sit here and have a cup of tea.

제임스 씨를 만나서 카페에 갔어요. I met James and went to the cafe.

빨리 호텔에 가서 쉬어야겠어요. I need to go hotel quickly and take a rest.

🍀 Complete the following dialogues as in the example.

> **Ex** 김밥을 만들어서 먹고 싶어요. (만들다)

(1) 어제 도서관에 _____ 한국어 공부를 했어요. (가다)

(2) 아침에 _____ 세수를 해요. (일어나다)

(3) 내일 친구를 _____ 쇼핑을 할 거예요. (만나다)

(4) 커피에 설탕을 _____ 마실 거예요. (넣다)

–(으)로² (direction)

'(으)로' is attached to a noun to indicate a direction of movement.

Nouns ending with a vowelor the consonant ㄹ → 로	Nouns ending with a consonant → 으로
회사 + 로 → 회사로 호텔 + 로 → 호텔로	식당 + 으로 → 식당으로 공항 + 으로 → 공항으로

지금 학교로 가요. I'm going to school now. 공항으로 가 주세요. Please go to the airport.

4번 출구로 나오세요. Come out from Exit 4. 위층으로 올라 가세요. Go upstairs.

라오스로 여행할 거예요. I will travel to Laos. 앞으로 쭉 가세요. Go straight.

♣ Answer the following questions as in the example.

> **Ex** A: 민수 씨, 지금 어디로 가요?
>
>   B: <u>학교로 가요.</u> (학교)

(1) A: 이번 휴가는 어디로 가요?

  B: _____. (푸켓)

(2) A: 이번 방학에 어디로 여행을 가고 싶어요?

  B: _____. (세부)

(3) A: 이 버스는 어디로 가요?

  B: _____. (강남역)

(4) A: 신혼여행은 어디로 갈 거예요?

  B: _____. (하와이)

A 실례지만 여기에서 관광객이 어디에 많이 가요?
Excuse me, but where do most tourists go here?

B 요즘은 바나힐 골든브릿지를 많이 가요.
The Golden Bridge at Ba Na Hills is popular these days.

A 여기에서 시간이 얼마나 걸려요?
How long does it take from here?

B 호텔에서 바나힐까지 택시로 5분쯤 걸립니다.
It takes about 5 minutes from the hotel to Ba Na Hills by a taxi.

혹시 걸어서 못 가요? Can't you walk to that place by any chance?

A 네, 할머니도 함께 가세요. 걸어서 못 가요. 멀어요.
Yes, grandma is coming with us. She can't go on foot. It's far away.

그럼 버스로 어떻게 가요? Then how can I get there by bus?

B 호텔 건너편 버스 정류장에서 버스를 타세요.
Take the bus at the bus stop across the hotel.

바나힐 앞에서 내리세요. 왼쪽에 골든 브릿지가 보일 거예요.
Get off in front of Ba Na Hills. You'll see the Golden Bridge on your left.

N1에서 N2까지

'N1에서 N2까지' comes after nouns that indicate places and indicates the departure point and the destination. When expressing the duration of some event, 'N1부터' and 'N2까지' are used to indicate the starting time and the ending time, respectively. 'N1에서 N2까지' and 'N1부터 N2까지' correspond to 'from N1 to N2' and 'from N1 until N2' in English. However, there's not much difference in the usage. You can usually use 'N1에서' and 'N1부터' interchangeably in most of the cases.

N1에서 N2까지
공항(N1) + 에서 호텔(N2) + 까지 → 공항에서 호텔까지
여기(N1) + 에서 환전소(N2) + 까지 → 여기에서 환전소까지

공항에서 호텔까지 택시로 왔어요. I came to the hotel from the airport by taxi.

여기에서 환전소까지 어떻게 가요? How can I get to the currency exchange from here?

이 식당은 오전 11시부터 오후 9시까지 열어요.
This restaurant is open from 11 a.m. to 9 p.m.

♣ **Complete the sentence as in the example.**

출발 Departure	도착 Arrival	소요 시간 Time required	교통 수단 Transportation
〈Ex〉 서울	부산	2시간 30분	KTX
(1) 부산	세부	4시간 20분	비행기
(2) 빈탄	싱가포르	1시간	배
(3) 서울	푸켓	6시간 20분	비행기
(4) 비엔티안	루앙프라방	2시간	기차

Ex 서울에서 부산까지 KTX로 2시 간 30분 걸려요

(1) _____.

(2) _____.

(3) _____.

(4) _____.

–이/가 걸리다

'이/가 걸리다' is used when expressing that something will take time. '–걸리다' is attached to the back of a word indicating time, indicating the time required to do something.

Nouns ending with a vowel → 이 걸리다	Nouns ending with a consonant → 가 걸리다
이십 분 + 이 → 20분이 걸려요	4시간 정도 + 가 → 4시간 정도가 걸려요

집에서 회사까지 버스로 20분이 걸려요. It takes 20 mins from my place to work by bus.
부산은 차로 4시간 정도가 걸려요. It takes about four hours by car to get to Busan.
공항에 가는데 한 시간이 걸려요. It takes an hour to get to the airport.

Complete the dialogues as in the example.

Ex A: 인천에서 방콕까지 얼마나 걸려요? How long does it take from Incheon to Bangkok?

B: <u>인천에서 방콕까지 6시간 걸려요.</u> (6시간)

(1) A: 호텔에서 공항까지 얼마나 걸려요?

How long does it take from the hotel to the airport?

B: _____. (2시간)

(2) A: 여기에서 야시장까지 얼마나 걸려요?

How long does it take to get to the night market from here?

B: _____. (30분)

(3) A: 루앙프라방에서 방비엥까지 얼마나 걸려요?

How long does it take from Luang Prabang to Vang Vieng?

B: _____. (4시간)

(4) A: 세부에서 보라카이까지 얼마나 걸려요?

How long does it take from Cebu to Boracay?

B: _____. (1시간)

못 + V

'못' attaches before a verb stem and is used when the subject has an intention to do something, but cannot do it because of his/her lack of ability or other external circumstances. It is equivalent to 'can't ~' in English.

-못 + V
못 + 가다 → 못 가다
못 + 먹다 → 못 먹다

다시 한번 말해 주세요. 못 들었어요. Can you say that again? I couldn't hear you.

저는 감기에 걸려서 집 밖에 못 나가요. Since I caught a cold, I can't go out of my house

늦잠을 자서 아침을 못 먹었어요. I couldn't have breakfast because I woke up late.

☞ For 'N하다' verbs, the noun is positioned before '못'.

공부하다: 공부 + 못 하다 → 공부 못 하다

운동하다: 운동 + 못 하다 → 운동 못 하다

☞ '못 V' and '안 V' are different in meaning.

제가 오늘 학교에 못 가요. I can't go to school today.

제가 오늘 학교에 안 가요. I don't go to school today.

♣ Complete the following dialogues as in the example.

Ex A: 전화를 받을 수 있어요?

B: 아니요, 전화를 못 받아요.

(1) A: 오늘 도서관에 가요?

B: _____ .

(2) A: 이번 주말에 친구를 만날까요?

B: _____ .

(3) A: 김치를 먹어요?

  B: _____ .

(4) A: 친구하고 한국말로 말해요?

  B: _____ .

Track 5-03

Dialogue 3 **Car rental** 렌터카 대여

A 어떻게 도와 드릴까요? How may I help you?

B 렌터카를 빌리고 싶어요. I'd like to rent a car.

A 잘 오셨습니다. 며칠 동안 필요하세요? Welcome. How many days do you need?

B 3일입니다. For three days, please.

A 빌리고 싶은 차 종류가 있으십니까? Do you have any particular car in mind?

B 부모님도 같이 탈 거예요. SUV로 빌리고 싶은데 추천 좀 해 주세요.
My parents will ride with me. I'd like to rent an SUV, so please recommend one.

A 아, 네. 물론이죠. 요즘 신형 SUV로 싼타페나 쏘렌토가 인기가 많습니다.
Oh, yes, of course. These days, Santa Fe and Sorrento are popular as new SUVs.

B 쏘렌토는 제가 작년에 운전했어요. 이번에는 다른 차로 빌리고 싶은데 카니발은 어때요?

I drove Sorento last year. I'd like to rent a different car this time, how about Carnival?

A 네, 준비해 드리겠습니다. Yes, I'll prepare it for you.

여권과 국제면허증 좀 보여주세요. Please show me your passport and international license.

보험도 가입하시겠어요? Would you like to buy insurance, too?

B 네, 그렇게 해 주세요. Yes, please.

Key Grammar 핵심 문법

–동안

'동안' is attached to a noun to Indicate the length of time starting when a certain action or behavior begins and lasting until it ends. It corresponds to 'during N / for N' in English.

–동안
휴가: 휴가 + 동안 → 휴가 동안
한 시간: 한 시간 + 동안 → 한 시간 동안

☞ After verb, '는 동안' is added to its stem as follows:

가다: 가 + 는 동안 → 가는 동안

읽다: 읽 + 는 동안 → 읽는 동안

휴가 동안(에) 뭘 할 거예요? What are you going to do during the vacation?

어제 12 시간 동안 잤어요.   I slept for 12 hours yesterday.

여행하는 동안 좋은 친구들을 많이 만났어요. I met many good friends while traveling.

✿ **Complete the following sentences using either '동안' or '는 동안' as in the example.**

....

Ex <u>시험을 보는 동안</u> 너무 긴장했어요. (시험을 보다)

(1) _____ 고향에 갈 거예요. (방학)

(2) 내가 _____ 동생은 텔레비전을 봐요. (책을 읽다)

(3) _____ 매일 비가 왔어요. (여행하다)

(4) _____ 한국어 공부를 했어요. (3년)

-(으)ㄴ데

'(으)ㄴ데' is attached to an adjective or a verb to express background situation for the second clause. It corresponds to 'so', 'therefore', 'and' or 'but' in English.

....

Adjective stem ending with a vowel or a consonant ㄹ → -ㄴ데	Adjective stem ends with consonant → -은데	For Verbs → -는데
바쁘다: 바쁘 + ㄴ데 → 아픈데	많다 : 많 + -은데요 → 많은데	먹다: 먹 + 는데 → 먹는데

....

심심한데 영화 보러 갈까요? I'm bored so shall we go to the movies?

날씨가 좋은데 산책하러 갈까요? The weather is nice so shall we go for a walk?

볼펜이 없는데 연필 드릴까요? I don't have a ballpoint pen so do you want a pencil?

맛집을 아는데 오늘은 문을 닫았어요. I know a good restaurant, but it's closed today.

♣ Complete the following sentences as in the example.

> **Ex** 덥다. 에어컨을 켜요. → <u>더운데 에어컨을 켜요.</u>

(1) 배가 고프다. 점심 먹으러 갈까요? → _____.

(2) 2년 동안 한국어를 배웠다. 아직 잘 못 해요. → _____.

(3) 머리가 아프다. 약국이 어디에 있어요? → _____.

(4) 비가 그쳤다. 같이 산책하러 가요. → _____.

–았/었/였

The past tense forms of adjectives and verbs are formed by adding '았', '었' or '였' to the stem of the word.

'–았어요' is attached to stems ending in the vowels ㅏ or ㅗ.	'–었어요' is attached to stems ending in other vowels.	'–했어요' is attached to stems ending in –하다.
살다: 살 + 았어요 → 살았어요 좋다: 좋 + 았어요 → 좋았어요	없다: 없 + 었어요 → 없었어요 배우다: 배우 + 었어요 → 배웠어요	공부하다: 공부 + 했어요 → 공부했어요

저는 필리핀에서 십년 동안 살았어요. I lived in Philippines for ten years.

지난 주말에는 날씨가 좋았어요. The weather was nice last weekend.

지갑에 돈이 없었어요. I didn't have any money in my wallet.

저는 작년에 운전을 배웠어요. I learned to drive last year.

어제 하루 종일 한국어 공부했어요. I studied Korean all day yesterday.

🍀 **Write complete sentences as in the example.**

....

> Ex   제임스 씨 / 지난 수요일 / 미국 / 가다 → <u>제임스 씨가 지난 수요일에 미국에 갔어요.</u>

(1) 제 친구 / 어제 / 한국 / 오다 → _____.

(2) 안나 씨 / 지난 주말 / 남대문 시장 / 쇼핑하다 → _____.

(3) 린 씨 / 3일 전 / 체육관 / 운동하다 → _____.

(4) 아랑 씨 / 어제 밤 / 노래방 / 노래 부르다 → _____.

4 Response Exercise 응답 연습

(**Location and direction** 위치와 방향

Track 5-04

A   이 버스가 호텔 앞에 가요? Does this bus go to the front of the hotel?

B   네, 갑니다. Yes, it does.

　　[아니요, 안 갑니다. 건너편에서 타세요.]

　　[No, it doesn't. Please take it across the street.]

A   리무진 버스는 어디에서 타요? Where can I take the limousine bus?

B   호텔 정문 앞에서 탑니다. You can take it in front of the main gate of the hotel.

A   호텔에 피트니스 센터가 있어요? Is there a fitness center in the hotel?

B   네, 아래층에 있습니다. 엘리베이터를 타고 내려 가세요.

　　Yes, it's downstairs. Take the elevator down.

A 시드니 하버 브릿지 방향을 알려주시겠어요?
Can you tell me the direction of Sydney Harbor Bridge?

B 두 블록 직진하셔서 좌회전 하세요. Go straight for two blocks and turn left.

A 방향 좀 물어도 될까요? Can I ask you for directions?

B 네, 그러세요. Yes, go ahead.

[저도 여기를 잘 몰라요.] [I don't know this place well either.]

Find a way & Moving on 길 찾기 & 이동하기

A 길을 찾도록 도와 주시겠어요? Could you help me find my way?

[길 좀 가르쳐 주시겠어요?] [Could you show me the way?]

B 이 지도에 표시를 해 드리겠습니다. Let me mark on this map.

[이 약도를 보고 설명해 드릴게요.] [Let me explain after looking at this map.]

A 가까운 지하철역을 가르쳐 주세요. Please tell me the nearest subway station.

B 이 지도에 표시를 해 드리겠습니다. Let me mark on this map.

A 지름길이 있나요? Is there a shortcut?

B 정문에서 보이는 시티타워 표지물을 보고 직진하세요.
Look at the City Tower sign seen from the main gate and go straight.

쉽게 찾을 수 있을 거예요. You'll find it easily.

A 우체국에 가려고 하는데 어떻게 가야 해요? How can I get to the post office?

B 횡단 보도를 건너면 우체국이 있어요. There's a post office across the crosswalk.

A 동대문 시장에 어떻게 가야 해요? How can I get to Dongdaemun Market?

B 동대문 시장역에서 내려서 2번 출구 쪽으로 나가면 상가가 많이 있어요.

If you get off at Dongdaemun Market Station and go out toward Exit 2, there are many shopping malls.

A 죄송합니다. 만나 식당에 가려고 하는데 좀 가르쳐 주실 수 있어요?

Excuse me. I'm going to the "Manna" restaurant. Could you tell me how to get there?

B 왼쪽에 있는 두 번째 골목으로 들어가면 그 식당이 있어요.

If you go into the second alley on the left, you will find the restaurant.

Means and Methods of Transportation 교통 수단과 방법

Track 5-06

A 어떻게 가요? How do I get there?

B 걸어서 갑니다. You can go on foot.

[버스로 가요.] You can go by bus.

A 시간이 얼마나 걸려요? How long does it take?

B 10분쯤요. About 10 minutes.

[10분쯤 돼요.] It's about 10 minutes.

[그때 그때 조금 달라요.] It varies a little from time to time.

A 거기까지 버스로 가는 것이 좋아요? 지하철로 가는 것이 좋아요?

Is it better to get there by bus or subway?

B 지하철로 가는 것이 좋습니다. You'd better take the subway.

A 죄송하지만 택시를 잡아 주시겠어요? Excuse me, but could you get me a taxi?

B 네, 알겠습니다. 로비 앞쪽에 서 계세요. Yes, I got it. Please stand in front of the lobby.

A 어디에서 갈아타야 돼요? Where should I transfer?

B 다음 역에서요. At the next station.

A 버스 시간표를 어디서 얻을 수 있을까요? Where can I get a bus schedule?

B 관광 안내소에서 받으실 수 있습니다. You can get it at the tourist information center.

Return of the rental car 렌터카 반납

Track 5-07

A 자동차를 빌리러 왔는데요. I'm here to rent a car.

B 운전면허증을 보여 주시겠어요? May I see your driver's license?

A 어떤 차종을 원하세요? What kind of car do you want?

B 가격표를 볼 수 있어요? 중형차를 원합니다. Can I see the price list? I want a medium-sized car.

[좀 저렴한 차가 좋겠어요.] [I want a bit cheaper car.]

A 차를 반납하고 싶습니다. I'd like to return the car.

B 손님, 계약서를 보여 주시겠어요? Sir, may I see the contract?

A 몇 시까지 반납해야 해요? By what time do I have to return it?

B 오전 11시까지 반납해 주세요. Please return it by 11 a.m.

[시간이 지나면 추가 요금을 내셔야 해요.]

[You will be charged additional fees for over time.]

A 어디에서 반납 하시겠어요? Where would you like to return it?

B 공항에서 반납해도 될까요? Can I return it at the airport?

Track 5-08

✅ Aspiration (격음화)

When the final consonant ㅎ is followed by the consonants ㄱ, ㄷ, ㅂ, ㅈ the pronunciations change as follows, ㄱ to [ㅋ], ㄷ to [ㅌ], ㅂ to [ㅍ] and ㅈ to [ㅊ]. In the above example, the initial consonant 'ㄱ' in '게' is connected to a final consonant 'ㅎ' in '떻' and 'ㄱ' is pronounced as 'ㅋ' to become [케] in the last syllable. Likewise, '좋다' is pronounced as [조타].

Ex   어떻게 → [어떠케]   그렇군요 → [그러쿤뇨]   입학 → [이팍]   백화점 → [배콰점]
      비슷하다 → [비스타다]

6 Additional Expression 추가 표현

A	▪ 10분 걸려요. It takes 10 minutes.
	◢ 10분이요. 10 minutes.
	◢ 10분쯤 걸려요. It takes about 10 minutes.
	◢ 10분 정도 걸립니다. It takes about 10 minutes.

A	▪ 며칠동안 필요하세요? How many days do you need?
	◢ 얼마동안 필요하세요? How long do you need it?
	◢ 얼마동안 사용하시겠어요? How long do you want to use it?
B	이틀 동안요. For two days, please.
	[2일이요.] [2 days, please.]

7.1 Transportation-related Culture 한국의 교통관련 문화

Public transportation in South Korea is exceptional. Home to 8 international airports, 6 domestic airports, the KTX and SRT high speed train networks, modern subway systems and one of the world's busiest sea ports, Korea boasts an abundance of stellar transportation options. At the local level, 6 Korean cities operate modern subway systems and all cities, large and small, have extensive bus routes. This combination makes it incredibly easy, and cost effective, to move around!

As of 2018, there are 348 stations for regular subways. The biggest advantage of the subway compared to other means of transportation is that it has the most number of people per hour. With 600 people on board, the hourly passenger traffic on the subway, which runs every two minutes during rush hour, is 18,000 people. The reason why the subway has the most number of people per hour because it uses a railroad. It can run at an average speed of 75 kilometers because there is nothing in the way of driving. The safety of the subway system is almost safe if checked regularly.

Buses are one of the most popular means of transportation in Korea. There are also types of buses, including city buses, intercity buses, and express buses. People pay the right fare by placing the transportation card on a card reader next to the bus driver. There is also a machine at a bus stop in Korea that allows passengers to check their remaining balance by bringing a transportation card such as T-money card that they want to use. In addition, the arrival time and remaining seats of the buses at the bus stop in question are displayed on the electronic display board, which is very convenient. If you search the desired bus number in the search box in conjunction with the Internet, you can find the arrival time of the bus, bus car number, etc., even if the passenger is not necessarily at the bus stop.

Taking a taxi in Korea is very convenient for international visitors, with an increasing num-

ber of taxi drivers being able to speak English. Taxis can be found at taxi stands in most busy city areas or hailed on the streets. There are also call taxis that can be requested by phone call or mobile application. However, tourists should note that call taxis start with a higher base fare than the taxis you flag down on the street. The base fare will vary by region, but taxis all use the same fare calculation of increase by time and distance traveled. While virtually all taxis operating in the Seoul area accept credit cards or transportation cards, it is possible that some taxis in the outlying or isolated regions may request cash only.

Standard taxis have different colors depending on their region; the standard taxis in Seoul are generally orange. The metropolitan areas and other cities feature many silver-colored standard taxis called "model taxi" in Korean. Deluxe taxis are black with a yellow sign on the top. Both sides of the taxi have the Deluxe Taxi sign. They offer slightly more passenger space and a higher standard of service than regular taxis. This means that the basic fare and the fare for additional distance are higher than regular taxis, but there is no late-night surcharge, excluding in Daegu. Deluxe taxis can generally be found at stands located in front of hotels, stations, bus terminals, and major city streets. A van taxi that can accommodate six to ten passengers is also available for larger groups. Jumbo taxis provide simultaneous interpretation by phone for certain languages, and are equipped with a receipt-issuing device and a credit card reader. Fares are the same as deluxe taxi. Because they are quite similar in appearance, a jumbo taxi can often be confused for a call van. A call van charges by size and volume of luggage, and negotiates taxi fare with passengers instead of charging by the meter. If you need a jumbo taxi, be sure to check for the jumbo taxi label on the side of the van.

7.2 Family relations and Addressing family members
한국인의 가족 관계와 호칭

The Korean family system is the center of society which was based on agriculture a long time ago. Koreans consider family and relatives important and addressing family members from the mother's and father's side is complicated. Before in Korea, there was the idea of nuclear families where children and their families would live with their parents and grandparents but in the present times, it is no longer practice. Nowadays, people would opt to live independently which is evident in the increasing number of single-person households in Korea. Despite this trend of living solo, family relations, gatherings, and the way to address family members are still considered important.

In Korea, family members usually include grandfathers and grandmothers, father and mother, and brothers/sisters. In addition, addressing family members vary depending on whether the person being addressed is a man, a woman, married, or not, or whether he/she is from the father's or mother's side of the family.

Due to the influence of traditional Confucian ideas, Koreans often use family names even in social relationships. In Korean, the meaning of "friend" in English is used to address family members such as "오빠 [girl's older brother], 언니 [girl's older sister], 누님 [boy's older sister], 형님 [boy's older brother]" depending on age or gender, and the level of intimacy. However, these ways of addressing family members should be used appropriately to avoid being rude and impolite to a family member being addressed.

Grandparents	조부모님	Maternal grandparents	외조부모님
Grandfather	할아버지	Grandmother	할머니
Maternal grandfather	외할아버지	Maternal grandmother	외할머니
Parents	부모님		
Father	아버지	Mother	어머니
Dad	아빠	Mom	엄마
Father's older brother	큰아버지	Father's older brother' wife	큰어머니
Father's younger brother	작은아버지	Father's younger brother's wife	작은어머니
Father's unmarried younger brother	삼촌	Mother's younger brother	외삼촌
Father's sister	고모	Mother's sister	이모
Big brother (if you are a boy)	형	Big brother (if you are a girl)	오빠
Big sister (if you are a boy)	누나	Big sister (if you are a girl)	언니
Younger brother	남동생	Younger sister	여동생
Brothers	형제	Sisters	자매

(1) 백화점 앞에 있어요.

(2) 커피숍 안에 있어요.

(3) 경찰서 뒤에 있어요.

(4) 만나 식당 건너편에 있어요.

(1) 가서   (2) 일어나서   (3) 만나서   (4) 넣어서

(1) 푸켓으로 가요.

(2) 세부로 여행을 가고 싶어요.

(3) 강남역으로 가요.

(4) 하와이로 갈 거예요.

(1) 서울에서 세부까지 비행기로 4시간 20분 걸려요.

(2) 빈탄에서 싱카포르까지 배로 1시간 걸려요.

(3) 서울에서 푸켓까지 비행기로 6시간 20분 걸려요.

(4) 비엔티안에서 루앙프라방까지 기차로 2시간 걸려요.

(1) 2시간 걸려요.

(2) 30분 걸려요.

(3) 4시간 걸려요.

(4) 1시간 걸려요.

(1) 아니요, 못 가요.

(2) 아니요, 못 만나요.

(3) 아니요, 못 먹어요.

(4) 아니요, 한국말로 말 못 해요.

(1) 방학동안   (2) 책을 읽는 동안   (3) 여행하는 동안   (4) 3년 동안

(1) 배가 고픈데 점심 먹으러 갈까요?

(2) 2년 동안 한국어를 배웠는데 아직 잘 못 해요.

(3) 머리가 아픈데 약국이 어디에 있어요?

(4) 비가 그쳤는데 같이 산책하러 가요.

(1) 제임스 씨가 어제 한국에서 왔어요.

(2) 안나 씨가 지난 주말 남대문 시장에서 쇼핑했어요.

(3) 린 씨가 3일 전에 체육관에서 운동했어요.

(4) 아랑 씨가 어젯밤 노래방에서 노래를 불렀어요.

6

오늘밤 공연 좌석은 매진됐습니다

The seats for tonight's show are sold out

Unit 6

오늘밤 공연 좌석은 매진됐습니다

The seats for tonight's show are sold out

---

1 Study Objectives 학습 목표

✎ To identify expressions used for viewing and field trips (체험과 견학, 탐방)

✎ To purchase or make reservation for a ticket (예매와 예약)

✎ To confirm the information of visiting places and tour etiquette.
(방문지 정보 확인과 에티켓)

✎ To use expressions related to concert halls and performance viewing
(관람과 소감)

---

2 Vocabulary 어휘

2.1 Dialogue Vocabulary 본문 어휘

Noun 명사

표 tickets	공연 performances	자리 / 좌석 seat
매진 sold out	가운데 center / the middle	뒤쪽 the back side
박물관 museum	소지품 personal belongings	줄 line
입구 entrance	사진 photo	촬영 photograph
플래쉬 flash	오디오 audio	가이드 guide

안내 guidance	책자 brochure	출입문 entrance door
스튜디오 studio	세트장 shooting location	기억 memory
주의사항 precautions	관리인 keeper	인형 doll
기념품 souvenir	가게 store	국립 national

Verb 동사

남다 remain	도착하다 arrive	들다 carry / pic up
사용하다 use	놓다 put	둘러보다 look around
구경하다 look around	개봉하다 unseal	서다 stand
돌아오다 come back		

Others 나머지

| 간단한 simple | 길다 long | 아쉽다 It's too bad |
| 항상 always | 대신에 instead | 빨리 quickly |

2.2 Related Vocabulary 관련 어휘

예약과 관람 Reservation and Viewing

관람 viewing	예약 reservation	예매 booking
출구 exit	비디오 video	돌아가다 go back
출발하다 depart / leave	앉다 sit	방문하다 visit
예약하다 make reservation		

공연 감상과 느낌 Appreciation and Impressions of Performance

| 감상하다 appreciate | 관람하다 see / watch | 신나다 be excited |
| 재미있다 interesting | 재미없다 dull | 놀라다 be amazed |

충격을 받다 be shocked	지루하다 boring	무섭다 scary
우습다 funny	유익하다 instructive	즐겁다 enjoyable
실망스럽다 disappointing	그저 그렇다 just so-so	천천히 slowly

3 Dialogue 대화

Track 6-01

Dialogue 1 **Reservation for a Performance** 공연 예약

A '캣츠' 표를 사고 싶은데요, 7시 공연에 남은 자리가 있나요?

I'd like to buy a ticket for 'Cats'. Do you have any seats left for the 7 o'clock performance?

B 오늘 밤 공연 좌석은 매진됐습니다. The seats for tonight's show are sold out.

A 그렇군요. 그럼, 3시 공연으로 가운데 자리 2개 있어요?

I see. Then, do you have two seats in the middle for the 3 o'clock performance?

B 아니요, 죄송하지만 지금은 뒤쪽 좌석만 남아 있습니다.

No, I'm sorry, but there are only back seats left.

-(으)ㄴ/는

'(으)ㄴ/는' is added to verbs or adjectives when used in front of a noun as a noun modifier.
For present tense adjective and past tense verbs, -(으)ㄴ is added to the stem.

'-은' is attached to the adjective stem or past tense verbs ends in a consonant other than 'ㄹ'	ㄴ' is attached to the adjective stem ends in a vowel or a consonant 'ㄹ'	-는 is added to the present tense verbs stem.
높다: 높 + 은 → 높은 먹다: 먹 + 은 → 먹(past tense)	예쁘다: 예쁘 + ㄴ → 예쁜 멀다: 머 + ㄴ → 먼	마시다: 마시 + 는 → 마시는

높은 산에 올라가고 싶어요. I want to climb a high mountain.

한식을 먹은 지 오래됐어요. It's been a long time since I had Korean food.

저는 예쁜 여자를 좋아해요. I like pretty woman.

꿀벌은 온종일 먼 거리를 여행해요. Honeybees travel long distance all day long.

커피를 마시는 사람이 제 친구예요. The person who drinks coffee is my friend.

🍀 **Write the correct forms of the words in parentheses in the blanks as in the example.**

Ex 높은 산 (높다)

(1) _____ 가방 (예쁘다)

(2) _____ 라면 (맵지 않다)

(3) _____ 책 (읽다: present tense)

(4) _____ 요리 (만들다: past tense)

–나요?

'나요?' attaches to a verb stem to ask politely and gently somebody a question. It is more commonly used by women than men as it gives a soft and famine feeling.

–나요?
되다: 되 + 나요? → 되나요?
도착했다: 도착했 + 나요? → 도착했나요? (Past tense)
있다: 있 + 나요? → 있나요?

한국어를 잘 하고 싶은데 어떻게 하면 되나요?
I want to be good at Korean, what should I do?

비행기가 제 시간에 도착했나요? Did the plane arrive on time?

이 근처에 화장실이 있나요? Is there a restroom around here?

♣ **Choose the appropriate word from below and fill in each blank using '–나요?' as in the example.**

있다 먹다 가시다 받았다 걸리다

Ex 언제 저녁을 <u>먹나요?</u>

(1) 내일 한국에 _____?

(2) 비자 연장하는 데 며칠이 _____?

(3) 이 근처에 약국이 _____?

(4) 이메일 주소를 휴대폰으로 _____?

-아/어/여 있다

'아/어/여 있다' attaches to a verb to indicate a person or an object is in a lasting static state. It corresponds to '-ed' or '-ing' in English. It is often used with passive verbs including '열리다', '닫히다', '켜지다', '꺼지다', '떨어지다' and '놓이다'.

'-아 있다' is attached to stems ending in the vowels ㅏ or ㅗ.	'-어 있다' is attached to stems ending in other vowels.
앉다: 앉 + 아 있다 → 앉아 있다 돌아오다: 돌아오 + 아 있다 → 돌아와 있다	꺼지다: 꺼지 + 어 있다 → 꺼져 있다 들다: 들 + 어 있다 → 들어 있다

참새들이 앉아 있어요. Sparrows are sitting down.

가로등이 꺼져 있어요. The streetlights are off.

식당이 닫혀 있어요. The restaurant is closed.

☞ Note that '아/어 있다' is used only with verbs that do not require a direct object.

의자가 넘어져 있어요. (O) The chair fell down.

의자를 넘어져 있어요. (x)

☞ Do not confuse with the progressive form '-고 있다'.

제임스가 산에 올라가고 있어요. James is climbing the mountain.

제임스가 산에 올라가 있어요. James is at the top of the mountain.

🍀 Write the correct forms of the words in parentheses using '아/어/여 있다' as in the example.

> Ex 창문이 <u>열려 있어요.</u> (열다)

(1) 아직 해야 할 일이 좀 _____. (남다)

(2) 무궁화 꽃이 _____. (피다)

(3) 책상 위에 책이 _____. (놓다)

(4) 지갑이 의자 밑에 _____. (떨어지다)

Dialogue 2   **Museum Tour** 박물관 견학

Track 6-02

A 이제 곧 국립박물관에 도착합니다.

We will arrive at the National Museum soon.

간단한 소지품만 들고 내리세요.

Please pick up your belongings only before getting off.

B 네, 그런데 가이드님, 저게 무슨 줄이에요 Yes, but guide, what line is that?

입구마다 줄이 너무 길어요. The line is too long at every entrance.

A 박물관 들어가는 줄입니다. It's the line for entering the museum.

여기는 항상 관광객이 많은 곳이에요. There are always many tourists here.

B 가이드님, 안에서 사진촬영을 해도 되나요?

Guide, can I take a picture inside?

A 네, 됩니다. 하지만 카메라 플래쉬를 사용하면 안 됩니다.

Yes, you can, but you're not supposed to use the camera flash.

B 한국말 오디오 가이드나 한국어 안내 책자가 있나요?

Is there a Korean audio guide or a Korean guidebook?

A 죄송하지만, 오디오 가이드는 없습니다.

I'm sorry, but we don't have an audio guide.

안내책자는 출입문 왼쪽에 놓여 있습니다.

The brochure is on the left side of the entrance.

Key Grammar 핵심 문법

–아/어/여도 되다

'아/어/여도 되다' attaches to a verb to express permission or approval for a behavior. It corresponds to 'may' or 'be allowed to' in English.

–아도 되다' is attached to stems ending in the vowels ㅏ or ㅗ.	'–어도 되다' is attached to stems ending in other vowels.	'–해도 되다' is attached to stems ending in –하다.
앉다: 앉 + 아도 되다 → 앉아도 되다	열다: 열 + 어도 되다 → 열어도 되다	전화하다: 전화 + 해도 되다 → 전화해도 되다

여기에 앉아도 돼요. You can sit here.

창문을 열어도 돼요? Can I open the window?

도서관에서 전화해도 돼요? Can I use a phone in the library?

♣ **Write the correct forms of the words in parentheses using** '아/어/여도 되다' **as in the example.**

Ex 박물관에서 <u>촬영해도 돼요.</u> (촬영하다)

(1) 이 컴퓨터 좀_____? (쓰다)

(2) 오늘 일찍 집에 _____. (가다)

(3) 밤에 _____? (전화하다)

(4) 내일 아침에 늦게 _____. (일어나다)

-(으)면 안 되다 ▸

'(으)면 안 되다' is attached to the stem of a verb or an adjective to express prohibition or restriction of an action or a state, which represents social conventions or common sense.

When the verb stem ends with a vowel and a consonant ㄹ → '안 되다'	When the verb stem ends with a consonant →'으면 안 되다'
피우다: 피우 + 면 안 되다 → 피우면 안 되다 전화하다: 전화하 + 면 안 되다 → 전화하면 안 되다	늦다: 늦 + 으면 안 되다 → 늦으면 안 되다 찍다: 찍 + 으면 안 되다 → 찍으면 안 되다

실내에서 담배를 피우면 안 돼요. Smoking indoors is not allowed.

밤에 전화하면 안 돼요. You shouldn't call at night.

약속 시간에 늦으면 안 돼요. Don't be late for an appointment.

이곳에서는 사진을 찍으면 안 돼요. You can't take pictures here.

♣ **Write the correct forms of the words in parentheses using** "(으)면 안 되다'
   as in the example.

> **Ex** 운전 중에 <u>전화하면 안 돼요.</u> (전화하다)

(1) 연필로 이 서류를 _____. (쓰다)

(2) 도서관에서 _____. (이야기하다)

(3) 수업 중에 전화를 _____. (받다)

(4) 쓰레기를 길에 _____. (버리다)

-마다

'마다' attaches to time nouns to express the repetition of the same or similar situation or behavior over a set period of time. It corresponds to 'every' or 'once every' in English. '마다' can also be added to the noun being described to indicate every one of something with no exceptions. In this case, it corresponds to 'every' or 'all' in English.

-마다
두 시간 + 마다 → 두 시간마다 호텔 + 마다 → 호텔마다

공항 가는 버스는 두 시간마다 와요. The bus to the airport comes every two hours.

휴가철에는 호텔마다 방이 없어요.

There are no rooms in each hotel during the holiday season.

제주도는 가는 곳마다 너무 아름다워요. Jeju Island is very beautiful everywhere I go.

♣ **Choose the appropriate word from below and fill in each blank using** '마다' **as in the example.**

때 주말 백화점 방 손님

Ex 저는 <u>주말마다</u> 운동해요. I exercise every weekend.

(1) ＿＿＿＿＿＿＿＿ 의견이 달라요.

Each customer has a different opinion.

(2) ABC 호텔에는 ＿＿＿＿＿＿＿＿ 와이파이가 있어요.

ABC Hotel has Wi-Fi in each room.

(3) 저는 카페에 갈 ＿＿＿＿＿＿＿＿ 카페 라떼를 마셔요.

Whenever I go to a cafe, I drink cafe latte.

(4) ＿＿＿＿＿＿＿＿ 사람이 많아요.

There are many people in each department store.

A 자, 여기가 유니버설 스튜디오입니다. 이제 내리시면 됩니다.

Well, this is Universal Studios. You can get off now.

B 와, 세트장이 굉장히 크네요. 사진에서 본 기억이 나요.

Wow, the shooting location is huge. I remember seeing it in the picture.

A 지금부터 스튜디오를 둘러보실 거예요.

We're going to look around the studio from now on.

구경하시기 전에 말씀드린 주의사항을 잘 지켜 주세요.

Please follow the precautions I told you before you look around.

B 저기요, 세트장 안으로 들어가도 되나요?

Excuse me, can I go into the shooting location?

A 들어가시면 안 돼요. 세트장마다 관리인이 있어요.

You can't go in. There's a keeper in every location.

사진과 비디오 촬영은 해도 됩니다.

You are allowed to take pictures and videos.

B 이런 구경은 처음이에요. 정말 멋져요.

I've never seen anything like this before. It's really cool.

A 모두 이쪽을 봐 주세요. 여기가 얼마 전에 개봉한 영화 '탑건'을 촬영한 곳입니다.

Please take a look here, everybody. This is where the movie "Top Gun" was recently filmed.

B 와, 정말 그렇네요. 오늘도 여기에서 영화 촬영을 하나요?

Wow, that's for sure. Is anyone also shooting a movie here today?

A 아쉽지만 오늘 촬영은 없습니다.

Unfortunately, there is no filming today.

대신에 구경할 시간을 좀 더 드릴까요?

Would you like to have a little more time to look around instead?

B 네, 좋아요. 우리도 저기 미니언즈 인형이 서 있는 기념품 가게로 빨리 가요.

Yeah, that's good. Let's go quickly to the souvenir shop where the Minions doll is standing.

A 그럼, 관람시간을 1시간 더 드리겠습니다. 4시까지는 버스로 돌아오셔야 합니다.

Then, I'll give you one more hour to look around. You have to come back to the bus by 4 o'clock.

Key Grammar 핵심 문법

-기 전에

'기 전에' attaches to verb stem to express the meaning of 'before some action'. It corresponds to 'before' in English.

-기 전에
자다: 자 + 기전에 → 자기 전에 먹다: 먹 + 기전에 → 먹기 전에

자기 전에 이를 닦으세요. Brush your teeth before you go to bed.

밥을 먹기 전에 손을 씻어요. Wash your hands before you eat.

수영하기 전에 준비운동을 해요. I do warm-up exercises before swimming.

🍀 **Choose the appropriate word from below and fill in each blank using** '기 전에' **as in the example.**

도착하다 보다 먹다 오다 체크 아웃하다

Ex 밥을 <u>먹기 전에</u> 손을 씻으세요.

(1) 호텔에서 _____ 방을 확인하세요.

(2) 공항에 _____ 연락주세요.

(3) 영화를 _____ 친구를 만났어요.

(4) 한국에 _____한국어를 배웠어요.

-아/어/여야 하다(되다)

'아/어/여야 하다' or '아/어/여야 되다' is added to the verb stem to express the meaning of "one has to…" or "one must…"

'-아야 하다/되다' is attached to stems ending in the vowels ㅏ or ㅗ.	'-어야 하다/되다' is attached to stems ending in other vowels.	'해야 하다/되다' is attached to stems ending in -하다.
가다: 가 + 아야 하다/되다 → 가야 하다/되다 오다: 오 + 아야 하다/되다 → 와야 하다/되다	먹다: 먹 + 어야 하다/되다 → 먹어야 하다/되다 쉬다: 쉬 + 어야 하다/되다 → 쉬어야 하다/되다	전화하다: 전화 + 해야 하다/되다 → 전화해야 하다/되다 예약하다: 예약 + 해야 하다/되다 → 예약해야 하다/되다

시간이 없어요. 빨리 가야 돼요. We don't have time. We need to go quickly.

늦지 마세요. 2시까지 버스로 와야 해요.

Don't be late. You have to come by bus by 2 pm.

현금이 없어서 카드를 써야 돼요. I have to use my card because I don't have cash.

아파요? 그럼 약을 먹어야 해요. Are you sick? Then, you have to take medicine.

호텔에 도착하면 부모님께 전화해야 돼요.

I have to call my parents when I get to the hotel.

내일 생일 파티가 있어요. 식당을 예약해야 해요.

There's a birthday party tomorrow. I need to make a reservation for a restaurant.

🍀 **Choose the appropriate word from below and fill in each blank using** '아/어/여 하다/되다' **as in the example.**

> 조용히 하다   타다   가다   출발하다   매다

Ex 친구가 서울에 와서 서울역에 <u>가야 돼요.</u>

(1) 버스가 안 와서 택시를 _____.

(2) 도서관에서 _____.

(3) 운전할 때는 안전벨트를 _____.

(4) 공항에 2시까지 가려면 지금 _____.

4 Response Exercise 응답 연습

Announcement upon arrival at the destination 방문지 도착과 공지

Track 6-04

A 목적지에 도착했습니다. 저를 따라오세요.
We've arrived at our destination. Please follow me.

[제 깃발을 따라오세요, 제가 안내해 드릴게요.]
[Please follow my flag, I'll show you around.]

[지금부터 저를 따라오세요. 이동합니다.]
[Please follow me from now on. We'll be moving on.]

B 네, 알겠습니다. Yes, sir/ma'am.

A 여기에서 얼마나 머물러요? How long do we stay here?

B 1시간 정도요. 1시 30분까지 버스로 돌아와 주세요.
About an hour. Please come back to the bus by 1:30.

버스는 한 시간 뒤에 다시 옵니다. The bus will come back after an hour.

[두 시간 후에 분수 앞에서 만나요.]
[Let's meet in front of the fountain after two hours.]

A 언제까지 돌아와야 하나요?
What time are we supposed to be back?

B 출발 15분 전까지 오셔야 합니다.
You have to be here 15 minutes before departure.

A 어디에서 입장권을 살 수 있어요? Where can I(We) buy an admission ticket?

B 정문 옆 매표소에서 사면 됩니다.
You can buy it at the ticket office next to the main gate.

A 지금 표를 살 수 있을까요? Can we buy tickets now?

B 그 영화는 매진되었습니다. The movie tickets are sold out.

A 외국인을 위한 할인이 있어요? Is there a discount for foreigners?

B 학생과 노인은 2달러씩 할인해 드립니다.
We offer a $2 discount for students and senior citizens.

A 표는 얼마죠? How much is the ticket?

B 티켓은 15달러이고 세금은 별도입니다. Tickets are $15 and tax is not included.

A 제 자리가 어디예요? Where is my seat?

B 2층 B열 15번 좌석입니다. It's seat number 15 in row B on the 2nd floor.

A 공연 시간이 어떻게 돼요? What time is the show/performance?
[공연은 얼마나 오래 하죠?] [How long does the performance last?]
[공연 시간이 얼마 동안이에요?] [How long does the performance last?]

B 공연 시간은 2시간입니다. The performance time is two hours.
[공연은 2시간 정도 합니다.] [The performance is about two hours long.]
[공연 시간은 2시간쯤 돼요.] [The performance is about two hours long.]

A 오늘 프로그램은 뭐예요? What's today's program?

B 사이먼 카바레 쇼입니다. It's the Simon Cabaret Show.

A 몇 시에 시작해요? What time does it begin?

B 15분 뒤에 시작합니다. It starts after 15 minutes.

A 언어 서비스가 제공되나요? Is language service available?

[오디오 가이드를 듣고 싶은데요.] [I want to listen to the audio guide.]

B 여기에서 대여하면 됩니다. 2달러입니다. You can rent it here. It's two dollars.

A 한국어 팸플릿이 있나요? Is there a Korean pamphlet?

B 네, 그리고 음성 안내기도 있어요. Yes, and there's also a voice guide.

A 공연은 어느 나라 말로 나와요? What language is the performance in?

B 영어로 나옵니다. It comes out in English.

[영어 대사입니다.] [It's an English line.]

[영어입니다.] [It's English.]

A 영어 자막이 나오나요? Are there English subtitles?

B 아니요, 영어 자막이 없습니다. No, there are no English subtitles.

[아니요, 따로 영어 자막은 없습니다.] [No, there are no English subtitles]

[네, 측면 비디오 화면에는 영어자막이 나옵니다.]

[Yes, there are English subtitles on the side video]

A 중간에 쉬는 시간이 있어요? Is there a break time in the middle of the show?

B 네, 있습니다. Yes, there is.

[네, 1부 끝나고 15분 휴식시간이 있습니다.]

[Yes, there's a 15-minute break after Part 1.]

[네, 중간에 쉬는 시간 10분 있습니다.] [Yes, you have 10 minutes to rest.]

[아니요, 쉬는 시간이 없습니다.] [No, there's no break time.]

A 누가 출연하나요? Who will be on the movie?

B 브래드 피트와 안젤리나 졸리가 나옵니다. It stars Brad Pitt and Angelina Jolie.

A 여기서 비디오 촬영 해도 돼요? Can I shoot a video here?

B 아니요, 안됩니다. No, you can't.

[죄송하지만, 비디오 촬영은 할 수 없습니다.] [Sorry, but you can't film a video]

A 음료를 가지고 안에 들어가도 될까요? Can I go inside with a drink?

B 아니요, 음료는 가지고 들어갈 수 없습니다. No, you can't bring drinks with you.

[죄송하지만, 여기에서 마시고 들어가야 해요.] [Sorry, but you have to drink here before entering.]

5 **Pronunciation** 발음

 Liaison (연음)

Track 6-07

When a syllable with a final consonant is followed by a syllable that begins with a vowel, the final consonant is pronounced together with the first vowel of the succeeding syllable.

When the double final consonant is followed by a vowel, only the second part of the double final consonant is moved to be the initial consonant of the next syllable. In the above example, when the second final consonant ㅎ in [찮] is followed by a vowel ㅏ in [아], ㅎ is dropped accordingly. Then the first final consonant ㄴ in [찮] is pronounced as if it is the initial consonant of the next syllable [아]. So 괜찮아요 is pronounced as [괜차나요].

Ex
책이 → [채기]   이름은 → [이르믄]   무엇을 → [무어슬]
수업이 → [수어비]   일본에서 → [일보네서]   괜찮아요 → [괜차나요]
들으세요 → [드르세요] 읽어요 → [일거요]   있어요 → [이써요]
넓어요 → [널버요]   직업 → [지겁]   얼음 → [어름]
할아버지 → [하라버지] 한국어 → [한구거]   음악 → [으막]
일요일 → [이료일]

6   Additional Expression 추가표현

A

▣ 오늘밤 공연 좌석은 매진됐습니다.

The seats for tonight's performance are sold out.

◲ 오늘밤 공연은 매진입니다. Tonight's performance is sold out

◲ 공연 좌석이 매진이에요. 자리가 없습니다.

The seats for performance are sold out. There are no seats available.

A

▣ 여기에서 얼마나 머물러요? How long do you stay here?

◲ 여기에서 얼마동안 있어요? How long would you be here?

◲ 여기에서 얼마나 있나요 How long would you be here?

A

▣ 사진을 찍어도 돼요? Can I take a picture?

B

◲ 사진을 찍으면 안 됩니다. You are not allowed to take pictures.

◲ [사진 촬영 금지예요.] [Taking pictures is prohibited.]

◲ [사진 촬영하시면 안 됩니다.] [You can't take pictures.]

7 Culture of Korea

7.1 Newly coined words that express the feelings of Koreans
한국 사람들의 감정 표현 신조어

짱이다

'짱' means "the best, awesome, great or amazing". '짱' is the exclamation that something is extraordinarily good. If someone does a favor, we can reply with "짱이다!". This is pretty much exclaiming that we're extremely appreciative of them and their action was extraordinary.

딱이에요

It's an expression that you use when you're looking for something that fits exactly what you need in a situation, and it's usually used more in speech than in writing. It corresponds to "(right) in line with ~" in English.

대박!

대박 means "awesome", "great", "killer", or "amazing". It is often used when you're dumbfounded by a situation, but it can also be used to say "대박나세요" meaning "I wish you great success!" to wish someone good luck. The word 대박 is used often between friends and can also be seen on advertisements. It is basically a noun and can be used with several verbs. "대박+ 이다 (to be)" means "to be awesome" and "대박+나다 (to come out)" means "to become successful" or "to be a hit (product)". Sometimes, however, 대박 can be used as an adverb, as in "대박 멋있다 (really cool)".

최애

최애 is a standard word in the Standard Korean Dictionary, which means 'love the most'. Originally, it was not used widely by the public, but the term "최애캐 [favorite character]" used in animation fandom has been transferred to the Korean idol fandom world and has become widely used as an abbreviation for "favorite." It is used to point to an object that one really likes and loves as the "best" and is sometimes expressed as "최애한다"

비추

Originally, 비추 was a neutral expression for non-recommendation, but one Internet site created a button that was not recommended as a button that functions opposite to the recommendation button, and accordingly, it became a word for opposition. Except for Internet community sites, the word "opposition" originally acted on behalf of this meaning, but with the development of Internet bulletin boards, the word "recommendation" became stronger, and it was not recommended as an opposition. It refers to things that are not satisfactory or recommended, restaurants, and places, and on the contrary, there is also a word 강추 which means "highly recommended."

득템

득템 is originally a term used in video games. 득 means "to get" or "to gain", and 템 comes from 아이템 (item). Just because you "get" an item, however, doesn't mean you have actually done 득템. 득템 is only used when you've gotten something that is either rare or high in value. For example, if you are looking for a particular piece of clothing or an electronic device that you have really wanted for a long time, and you finally bought it, you can use the verb 득템하다. Over time, 득템 has also come to mean that someone has gained something through luck, but in a sarcastic manner.

가심비

It means psychological satisfaction compared to the price, and when the price is expensive but the satisfaction you feel is high, the expression "가심비가 좋다" is used. It is often used in words contrary to 가성비 and shows a difference in that it is based on mental satisfaction, not price. Since one's satisfaction is literally important in 가심비, first impressions of the object and social reputation can affect it.

고고씽

고고씽 or 고고싱 means "Let's go!" or "Let's do it!" The word "고" comes from the English word "go" (and it is repeated in this phrase), while "씽" comes from the Korean expression "씽씽" which describes the way an object or a person moves at a fast speed. As 고고씽 means "Let's go somewhere." or "Let's hurry up and start.", it is used with excitement and cheerful feeling. If someone suggests doing something and you want to express your agreement, you can say "고고씽".

맛저

맛저 is a newly coined word that has been used since 2014 and is a short form of '맛있는 저녁 [delicious dinner]'. It is usually said that '맛있는 저녁하세요. [Have a delicious dinner.]'. It is a meal greeting that is used in a friendly and affectionate manner for people in close relationships. Likewise, 맛점 is used to express '맛있는 점심 [delicious lunch]'.

7.2 Four seasons and seasonal activities & festivals in Korea
한국의 4계절과 계절활동 & 축제

Korea has four distinct seasons: spring, summer, fall, and winter. Spring is a season where warm and beautiful flowers bloom from March to May. So, there are many flower festivals during spring in Korea such as the Jeju Canola Flower Festival on Jeju Island, the Gunhang Festival, and the Cherry Blossom Festival in Jinhae which are worth seeing.

Summer is usually hot and rainy from June to August. The rainy season is experienced at the beginning of summer. After the rainy season, the temperature rises, and hot weather with high humidity continues. People usually leave the city and go on vacation or travel to beaches or cool valleys to avoid the heat. There are many sea festivals in summer in areas along the sea. Busan's sea festival is famous and Boryeong Mud Festival is also worth visiting.

Autumn is from September to November, and you can see blue skies and beautiful autumn leaves in cool weather. People visit the mountains a lot to enjoy the clear and refreshing autumn weather and see autumn leaves. There are many mountains in Korea. These mountains reveal different beauty from season to season due to the distinct Korean weather. Koreans also enjoy hiking because they can easily find mountains nearby without having to go far. There is Naejangsan Mountain Maple Festival, which is famous for viewing autumn leaves, while chrysanthemum festivals are held everywhere. Winter is windy in cold and dry weather from December to February. Snowflake festivals are celebrated in Daegwallyeong, Gangwon-do, and Hallasan, Jeju-do when the average temperature falls below zero and the snowy winter comes.

Koreans tend to focus on spending time with their families on weekends and vacations. Meanwhile, leisure activities and outdoor sports for families are also popular. Highway traffic congestion is common during holidays and vacation seasons as more and more people visit famous tourist attractions and festivals across the country. Recently, as the implementation of the five-day workweek has expanded, hobby activities and various self-development activities to improve health have been increasing.

7.3 Koreans' favorite hobby 한국인이 좋아하는 취미

Koreans are fond of doing different things as a hobby, so it's hard to indicate a single hobby. They enjoy outdoor activities like playing sports, hanging out at coffee shops, or shopping. However, indoor activities like watching Korean dramas or movies, texting their friends, and eating good food are highly enjoyed by many too. Listening to Korean pop music by popular Korean artists is a hobby many people enjoy.

Korea has beautiful parks all around that you can visit for an evening stroll or sightseeing, especially during the Spring when the flowers bloom and during Autumn to witness the Autumn foliage. In busy places like Seoul, parks are usually very crowded, but if you live in cities with less population like Songdo, you will find many attractive parks almost empty. There are many enjoyable activities to do at parks, and you will find people walking, jogging, cycling, riding boats, working out, eating, or just sightseeing. Families and friends spend sunny afternoons together on picnics having quality time with each other, playing games, and enjoying delicious food.

Hiking mainly on weekends is another favorite Korean leisure time activity, especially among the older generation. It is an excellent way to explore the gorgeous mountainous country. Hiking is considered the most popular pastime activity among Koreans, which is attributed to their competitive nature. They invest in hiking gear and take time off to hike the mountains whenever they can. Hiking goes hand in hand with camping, especially during the summer as friends and families enjoy a peaceful retreat in designated camping sites in Korea. These interests are just a few, and there are plenty more things that are fun to do for Koreans.

🖈 **Dialogue 1**

(1) 예쁜 가방　　(2) 맵지 않은 라면　　(3) 읽는 책　　(4) 만든 요리

(1) 오나요.　　(2) 걸리나요.　　(3) 있나요.　　(4) 받았나요.

(1) 남아 있어요.　(2) 피었어요.　　(3) 놓여 있어요.　(4) 떨어져 있어요.

🖈 **Dialogue 2**

(1) 써도 돼요.　　(2) 가도 돼요.　　(3) 전화해도 돼요.　　(4) 일어나도 돼요.

(1) 쓰면 안 돼요.　　　　(2) 이야기하면 안 돼요.
(3) 받으면 안 돼요.　　　　(4) 버리면 안 돼요.

(1) 손님마다　　　(2) 방마다　　　(3) 때마다　　　(4) 백화점마다

🖈 **Dialogue 3**

(1) 체크 아웃하기 전에　　　(2) 도착하기 전에
(3) 보기 전에　　　　　　　(4) 오기 전에

(1) 타야 해요(돼요).　　　　(2) 조용히 해야 해요(돼요).
(3) 매야 해요(돼요).　　　　(4) 출발해야 해요(돼요).

메모

7

스노클링을 해 본 적이 있으세요?

Have you ever snorkeled?

Unit 7

스노클링을 해 본 적이 있으세요?
Have you ever snorkeled?

---

1 Study Objectives 학습 목표

✎ To know expressions related to package tours and sightseeing
  (패키지 여행과 관광)

✎ To use expressions related to recommending famous tourist places and introducing tour packages (유명여행지 추천과 관광상품 안내)

✎ To participate in various outdoor activities and photography
  (다양한 야외 활동과 사진 촬영)

✎ To know how to introduce and use tourist facilities (관광 시설 소개와 이용)

---

2 Vocabulary 어휘

2.1 Dialogue Vocabulary 본문 어휘

Noun 명사 ✎

스노클링 snorkeling	해변 beach	명소 attraction
자유시간 free time	관광지 tourist attraction	관심 interest
야시장 night market	거리 distance	태국 Thailand
길거리 street	해산물 seafood	야간 night time

(대)관람차 large Ferris wheel	강변 riverside	맥주 beer
기념품 souvenir	배경 background	버튼 button
사원 temple / mosque	포토존 photo zone	김치 kimchi
소나기 shower	천둥 thunder	번개 lightning

Verb 동사

찾다 find	배우다 learn	즐기다 enjoy
추천하다 recommend	맛보다 taste	머무르다 stay
찍다 shoot	누르다 press	

Others 나머지

크다 big	유명하다 famous	신선하다 fresh
시원하다 cool	금방 soon	편하게 easily
천천히 slowly		

2.2 Related Vocabulary 관련 어휘

여행과 여행지 Travel and Destination

광장 square / plaza	놀이동산 amusement park	동물원 zoo
목적지 destination	바다 sea	바닷가 beach / coast
박물관 museum	산 mountain	섬 island
스키장 ski resort	식물원 botanical garden	온천 hot spring
유적지 historic site	캠핑장 camping site	폭포 waterfalls
호수 lake	휴양지 vacation spot	관광안내서 travel brochure
싣다 load(a luggage/cargo)	국내 여행 domestic trip	단체 여행 group tour
도보 여행 walking tour	렌터카 rental car	배낭여행 backpacking trip

배표 ship ticket	비행기표 air ticket	신혼여행 honeymoon
입장료 admission fee	성수기 high season	비수기 low season
자유 여행 free travel	축제 festival	피서지 summer resort
해외여행 overseas trip	효도 관광 filial tour	특산물 regional specialty
패키지 상품 travel packages		

야외 활동과 사진 촬영 Outdoor Activities and Photography

사진 촬영 photo shoot	즉석 사진 instant photo	파노라마 panorama
야경 night view	초점 focus	셔터 shutter
눈을 감다 blink	웃어요 Say cheese	초점이 맞지 않은 out of focus
사진을 찍다 take a picture	구경하다 sightsee	이국적 exotic
인상적 impressive	둘러보다 look around	유명하다 famous
찾아다니다 look for	체험하다 experience	호텔에 묵다 stay a hotel

비디오를 촬영하다 to film a video

하루 더 머물다 stay one more night

좋은 추억이 되다 be a nice memory

기억에 남다 remain in one's memory

볼거리가 풍성하다 be full of things to see

피서를 가다 go on a summer vacation

짐을 싸다 pack one's things (belongings)

인심이 좋다 be generous, be warm-hearted

산 정상에 오르다 get to the top of a mountain 거리를 돌아다니다 wander about in the streets

여행 일정을 잡다/세우다 arrange/schedule a tour

가벼운 옷차림으로 가다 go wearing light clothes

민박을 하다 stay at a homestay, lodge temporarily

노점상을 구경하다 take a look at the street vendors

기후와 날씨 Climate and Weather

흐린 overcast	따뜻한 warm	선선한 cool
더운 hot	추운 cold	맑은 clear

화창한 sunny	구름 낀 cloudy	가랑비 내리는 drizzly
비가 오는 rainy	바람부는 windy	눈이 내리는 snowy
후덥지근한 muggy	습기 찬 humid	축축한 wet
안개 낀 foggy		

3 Dialogue 대화

Dialogue 1 **Guide to tourist products** 관광 상품 안내

Track 7-01

A 와, 여기에는 스노클링하는 사람들이 많네요.
Wow, there's a lot of snorkeling people here.

B 네, 리티디안 해변은 관광객들이 많이 찾는 스노클링 명소예요.
Yes, Littidian Beach is a popular snorkeling spot.

안나 씨는 스노클링을 해 본 적이 있으세요? Anna, have you ever snorkeled?

A 아니요, 한번도 해 본 적이 없는데, 저도 할 수 있을까요?
No, I've never done it before and do you think I can do it, too?

B 물론이죠. 금방 배울 수 있습니다. Of course. You can learn it quickly.

점심 식사가 끝난 후에 자유시간이 있어요. 그때 즐겨 보세요.

You have free time after lunch. Please enjoy it then.

Key Grammar 핵심 문법

-(으)ㄴ 적이 있다/없다

This pattern is always attached directly to the end of a verb stem. It is used to express having or not having a particular experience in the past. It corresponds to "have / haven't had the experience of ~" in English. '(으)ㄴ 적이 있다' can also be used in the question form to express 'have you ever ~ ?' It is often combined with the form 'V + 아/어 보다' to ask someone if they've ever tried something. The opposite pattern is '(으)ㄴ 적이 없다'.

When the verb stem ends with a vowel and a consonant ㄹ → -ㄴ 적이 있다/없다	When the verb stem ends with a consonant → -은 적이 있다/없다
가다: 가 + ㄴ 적이 있다 → 간 적이 있다 실수하다: 실수하 + ㄴ 적이 있다 → 실수한 적이 있다 만들다: 만드 + ㄴ 적이 없다 → 만든 적이 없다 (* Final consonant 'ㄹ' is dropped.)	먹다: 먹 + 은 적이 있다 → 먹은 적이 있다 듣다: 듣 + 은 적이 없다 → 들은 적이 없다 (* 'ㄷ' irregular)

저는 제주도에 간 적이 있어요. I've been to Jeju Island.

한국말을 몰라서 실수한 적이 있어요. I've made a mistake because of my poor Korean.

저는 김치를 만든 적이 없어요. I've never made kimchi.

불고기를 먹은 적이 있어요? Have you ever eaten bulgogi?

민수? 그 이름을 들은 적이 없는 것 같아요.

Min-Su? I don't think I've ever heard that name.

🍀 **Ask and answer the questions about experiences as in the example.**

> **Ex** 필리핀에 가다. → A: 필리핀에 간 적이 있어요?
> B: 네, 필리핀에 간 적이 있어요.
> C: 아니요, 필리핀에 간 적이 없어요.

1) 한국어 수업에 결석하다. → A: _____

                                            B: _____

                                            C: _____

2) 휴대 전화를 잃어버리다. → A: _____

                                            B: _____

                                            C: _____

3) BTS를 만나다. → A: _____

                             B: _____

                             C: _____

4) K-pop을 듣다. → A: _____

                             B: _____

                             C: _____

−아/어/여 보다

'−아/어/여 보다' is used to indicate trying to do something. When used in the past tense (−아/어/여 봤어요), it can refer to whether something has been attempted. To express not having attempted, '못 V−아/어/여 봤어요' pattern is used.

'−아 보다' is attached to stems ending in the vowels ㅏ or ㅗ.	'−어 보다' is attached to stems ending in other vowels.	'해 보다' is attached to stems ending in −하다.
가다: 가 + 아 보다 → 가 보다	먹다: 먹 + 어 보다 → 먹어 보다	운전하다: 운전 + 해 보다 → 운전해 보다

서울에 가 봤어요. I've been to Seoul.

A: 오토바이를 운전 해 봤어요? Have you ever driven a motor bike?

B: 아니요, 못 해 봤어요. No, I haven't.

김치를 먹어 봤어요. I've eaten kimchi.

🍀 **Ask and answer the questions about experiences as in the example.**

Ex 편의점에서 아르바이트를 하다. → A: <u>편의점에서 아르바이트를 해 봤어요?</u>
B: <u>네, 해 봤어요.</u>
C: <u>아니요, 못 해 봤어요.</u>

1) 불고기를 먹다. → A: _____

B: _____

C: _____

2) 어릴 때 피아노를 배우다. → A: _____

                                                    B: _____

                                                    C: _____

3) 유명한 운동 선수를 만나다. → A: _____

                                                    B: _____

                                                    C: _____

4) 바다에서 수영을 하다. → A: _____

                                                    B: _____

                                                    C: _____

–(으)ㄹ 수 있다/없다

'(으)ㄹ 수 있다/없다' is used to express the possibility or ability. It corresponds to "can/cannot" in English. When someone is able to do something, or if there is possibility then '(으)ㄹ 수 있다' is used. When someone is not able to do something, or if there is no possibility then '(으)ㄹ 수 없다' is used. This pattern is also used to inquire about the possibility in the sense of requesting permission from someone.

When the verb stem ends with a vowel and a consonant ㄹ → '-ㄹ 수 있다/없다'	When the verb stem ends with a consonant → '-을 수 있다/없다'
만나다: 만나 + ㄹ 수 있다/없다 → 만날 수 있다/없다 만들다: 만들 + 수 있다/없다 → 만들 수 있다/없다	읽다: 읽 + 을 수 있다/없다 → 읽을 수 있다/없다 찍다: 찍 + 을 수 있다/없다 → 찍을 수 있다/없다

감기에 걸려서 오늘 만날 수 없어요. I can't meet you today because I have a cold.

한국 요리를 만들 수 있어요? Can you cook Korean food?

아랍어를 읽을 수 있어요? Can you read Arabic?

미술관에서 플래시 없이 사진을 찍을 수 있어요.

You can take pictures without flash at the art museum.

🍀 **Use the expressions in parentheses to complete the following dialogues as in the example.**

Ex A: 버스 안에서 커피를 마실 수 있어요? (버스 안에서 커피를 마시다)
   B: 아니요. 마실 수 없어요. (아니요)

1) A: _____ (매운 음식을 먹다)

   B: _____ (네)

2) A: _____ (한국어를 말하다)

   B: _____ (아니요)

3) A: _____ (한복을 혼자 입다)

   B: _____ (아니요)

4) A: _____ (오늘 저녁에 만나다)

  B: _____ (네)

Dialogue 2   **Recommendation to travel destination** 여행지 추천   Track 7-02

A   뭐 하나 물어봐도 될까요?   May I ask you a question?

B   그럼요, 말씀하세요.   Sure, go ahead.

A   근처에서 가 볼 만한 관광지 좀 추천해 주시겠어요?
Can you recommend any tourist attractions worth visiting nearby?

B   네, 물론이죠. 어떤 곳에 관심이 많으세요?
Yes, of course. What kind of places are you interested in?

A   야시장이나 젊은 사람들이 많이 찾는 거리를 구경하고 싶어요.
I want to see the night market or the streets that many young people visit.

B   그럼, 아시아티크 야시장을 한번 가 보세요.
Then, why don't you go to the Asiatique Night Market.

     태국 야시장 중에서 가장 크고 유명한 곳이에요.
It is the biggest and most famous place among Thai night markets.

A 와, 재미있겠는데요. 그럼 태국 길거리 음식도 맛볼 수 있을까요?

Wow, that sounds fun. Then can I taste Thai street food?

B 물론이죠. 길거리 음식도 많고 신선한 해산물도 먹을 수 있어요.

Of course. There are a lot of street food and you can also have fresh seafood.

야간에는 대관람차도 타고 짜오프라야 강변에서 시원한 맥주도 한잔 드셔 보세요.

At night, take a Ferris wheel and try a glass of cold beer along the Chao Phraya River, too.

Key Grammar 핵심 문법

-(으)ㄹ 만하다

There are four usages of '~(으)ㄹ 만하다' as follows.

1. It can imply a meaning of 'worth doing' and is used to give/ask for recommendations. Often used together with '정말'

서울의 인사동은 한번 구경할 만해요. Insadong in Seoul is worth visiting once.

이 식당은 정말 먹을 만해요. This restaurant is really worth visiting to eat.

다낭은 베트남에서 가 볼 만해요. Da Nang is worth visiting in Vietnam.

2. While the speaker is not completely satisfied, the action is still 'doable' or 'bearable'. Often used together with '아직' or '그냥'.

한국어는 배울 만해요? Is Korean worth learning?

이 가방은 아직 쓸 만해요. This bag is still usable.

아프지만 아직 참을 만해요. It hurts, but it's still bearable.

When the verb stem ends with a vowel and a consonant ㄹ → 'ㄹ 만하다'	When the verb stem ends with a consonant → '을 만하다'
사다: 보 + ㄹ 만하다 → 살 만하다 가다: 가 + ㄹ 만하다 → 갈 만하다	먹다: 먹 + 을 만하다 → 먹을 만하다 믿다: 믿 + 을 만하다 → 믿을 만하다

☞ In addition to describe the subject of a sentence, '(으)ㄹ 만하다' can also be used to describe an upcoming noun as an adjective.

....

먹을 만한 식당을 알아요?

Do you know a good restaurant worth visiting to eat?

세부에서 갈 만한 곳들을 좀 알려 주세요.

Please tell me some places worth going in Cebu.

살 만한 청바지가 있어요.

There are jeans that I want to buy (there are jeans that would be worthwhile buying).

믿을 만한 사람이 없어요.

There isn't anyone worth to trust.

🍀 **Use the words in parentheses to fill in the blanks in the following dialogues as in the example.**

....

Ex A: 이번 겨울에 필리핀으로 여행가면 어떨까요?
   B: 필리핀은 경치가 아름다워서 <u>여행을 갈 만해요</u>. (여행을 가다)

1) A: 일주일동안 동남아에 여행할 만한 나라가 있어요?
   B: 라오스는 물가가 싸서 _____. (추천하다)

2) A: 한국 드라마가 재미있다면서요?
   B: 네, 정말 _____. 한번 보세요. (보다)

3) A: 외국에서 손님이 오는데 어떤 음식을 대접하면 좋을까요?

　　B: 불고기나 갈비가 _____. (먹다)

4) A: 다음 주말에 남대문시장으로 쇼핑을 가면 어떨까요?

　　B: 남대문시장은 물건 가격이 싸서 _____. (쇼핑하다)

가장 -하다

'가장' is used to express superlative of an adjective in Korean. All you need to do is to add one word '가장' to the associated adjective.

　　유명한 famous → 가장 유명한 most famous

　　중요한 important → 가장 중요한 most important

A synonym of '가장' is '제일,' which is often used in speech. You can add this to the sentence before the adjective it modifies.

가장 -하다
유명하다: 가장 + 유명하다 → 가장 유명하다 중요하다: 가장 + 중요하다 → 가장 중요하다

제주도는 한국에서 가장 (제일) 유명한 관광지예요.

Jeju Island is the most famous tourist destination in Korea.

가족은 가장 (제일) 중요해요. Family is the most important.

이 호수는 세계에서 가장 (제일) 커요. This lake is the biggest lake in the world.

☞ '가장' can't be used with most verbs unless there is also an adverb included within the sentence.

　　나는 우리 팀에서 가장 달려요. (X)

　　나는 우리 팀에서 가장 빨리 달려요. (O) I run the fastest in our team.

However, '가장' can be added to '좋아하다 (to like)' without an adverb to indicate that you 'like something the most.'

나는 그 여자를 가장 좋아해요. I like that girl the most.

☞ Note here that in most real situations it is probably more natural to say as follows:

나는 우리 팀에서 가장 빨리 달려요. → 나는 우리 팀에서 가장 빨리 달리는 사람이에요. (√)

I'm the fastest runner in our team.

나는 그 여자를 가장 좋아해요. → 그 여자는 내가 가장 좋아하는 사람이에요. (√)

That woman is the person I like the most.

🍀 Fill in the blanks as in the example.

Ex 이 근처에서 <u>가장 가까운</u> 약국이 어디에 있어요? (가깝다)

(1) 필립 씨는 한국 음식 중에서 _____ 음식이 뭐예요? (좋아하다)

(2) 한국어 공부할 때 _____ 방법을 알려주세요. (효과적이다)

(3) 친구 중에서 _____ 친구가 누구예요? (친하다)

(4) 서울은 한국에서 _____ 도시예요. (크다)

-고[1]

'-고' is added to the stems of verbs and adjectives to list two or more actions, states, or facts. It corresponds to 'and' in English. '-고' is added to a verb stem or adjective stem to combine two sentences into one.

'–고' is attached to the verb, adjective, and 'noun+이다' of the sentence, and is used to connect the preceding and the latter sentences equally regardless of the order of time.

–고[1]
푸엉 씨는 호텔에 가요. + 안나 씨는 커피숍에 가요. → 푸엉 씨는 호텔에 가고 안나 씨는 커피숍에 가요. Phuong goes to the hotel and Anna goes to the coffee shop. 이 가방은 싸요. + (그리고) 이 가방은 예뻐요 → 이 가방은 싸고 예뻐요. This bag is cheap and pretty.

🍀 **Fill in the blanks using '–고' as in the example.**

> Ex　A: 한국어 책이 어때요? (쉽다, 재미있다)
> 　　B: 한국어 책이 쉽고 재미있어요.

1) A: 이 호텔이 어때요? (방이 넓다, 서비스가 좋다)

　　B: _____

2) A: 어디 아파요? (피곤하다, 졸리다)

　　B: _____

3) A: 내일 뭐 할 거예요? (빨래를 하다, 집안 청소를 하다)

　　B: _____

4) A: 오늘 날씨가 어때요? (맑다, 덥다)

　　B: _____

A 가이드님, 저희가 여기에서 얼마나 머물러요?

How long do we stay here, guide (Mr./Miss/Mrs.)?

B 2시간 정도입니다. 기념품 가게를 둘러본 후에 천천히 구경하시면 됩니다.

About two hours. You can take your time after looking around the souvenir shop.

A 저, 죄송한데 사진 좀 찍어 주시면 안 될까요?

Well, I'm sorry, but could you take a picture of me?

B 네, 찍어 드릴게요. 어떻게 찍어 드릴까요?

Yes, I'll take it for you. How do you like me to take it?

A 저 관람차를 배경으로 찍어 주시면 좋겠어요. 이 버튼만 누르면 돼요.

I'd like you to take a picture of that Ferris wheel in the background. Just press this button.

B 조금만 왼쪽에 서 보세요. 네, 좋아요. 찍습니다. 하나, 둘, 셋!

Please stand a little to the left. Okay, good. Here we go. 1, 2, 3!

A 정말 마음에 들어요. 감사합니다. 한번 보시겠어요?

I love it. Thank you. Would you like to take a look?

B 사진이 참 잘 나왔습니다. 배경도 멋지고 표정도 너무 좋으세요.

The picture came out really well. The background is cool and your look is so nice.

A 감사합니다. 저랑 사진 한 장 같이 찍으시겠어요?

Thank you. Would you like to take a picture with me?

B 좋습니다. 사원이 보이는 이 자리에서 괜찮으세요?

All right. Are you okay with this place where you can see the temple?

A 네, 그럼요, 여기가 포토존이에요? Of course, is this the photo zone?

B 맞아요. 이 사원에 대해 들어 보셨을 거예요. 이쪽에서 찍으면 더 예뻐요.

That's right. I'm sure you've heard about this temple. It'd be prettier if you take it from this side.

A 오, 좋아요. 제 휴대폰으로 찍을게요. '김치'하고 웃으세요.

Oh, that's great. I'll take it with my cell phone. Say "Kimchi" and smile.

Key Grammar 핵심 문법

-(으)ㄴ 후에

'(으)ㄴ 후에' is used when the speaker wants to express something 'after a certain time or action' and in general means "after (verb)ing."

When the verb stem ends with a vowel and a consonant ㄹ → 'ㄴ 후에'	When the verb stem ends with a consonant → '-은 후에'
쓰다: 쓰 + ㄴ 후에 → 쓴 후에 만들다: 만드 + ㄴ 후에 → 만든 후에	씻다: 씻 + 은 후에 → 씻은 후에 읽다: 읽 + 은 후에 → 읽은 후에

☞ This pattern cannot be used with past tense form '-았/었-'.

텔레비전을 봤은 후에 자요. (X)

텔레비전을 본 후에 잤어요. (O) I slept after watching TV.

이메일 주소를 쓴 후에 저에게 주세요.

Please give it to me after writing email address.

여권을 만든 후에 비행기표를 사요. I buy a plane ticket after I make a passport.

손을 씻은 후에 식사를 하세요. Please have a meal after washing your hands.

그는 저녁을 먹은 후에 잠이 드는 버릇이 있었다.

He had a habit of falling asleep after dinner.

🍀 **Create a sentence using "-(으)ㄴ 후에' as in the example.**

> Ex 학교를 졸업하다 / 취직하고 싶어요 → 학교를 졸업한 후에 취직하고 싶어요.

1) 점심을 먹다 / 커피를 마십시다 → _____

2) 호텔에 체크인하다 / 뭐 할 거예요? → _____

3) 계획을 세우다 / 여행을 하겠어요 → _____

4) 책을 읽다 / 산책을 할 거예요 → _____

🍀 **Complete the following dialogues using "-(으)ㄴ 후에' as in the example.**

> Ex A: 퇴근 후에 시간 있어요?
> B: 미안해요. 근무가 끝난 후에 친구와 약속이 있어요. (근무가 끝나다)

1) A: 어제 오후에 뭐 했어요?

   B: _____ 빨래를 했어요. (설거지를 하다)

2) A: 언제 잠을 잘 거예요?

   B: _____ 잘 거예요. (책을 다 읽다)

3) A: 한국 가는 비행기표를 샀어요?

   B: 아니요. _____ 살 거예요. (여권을 만들다)

4) A: 한국에 가면 연락주세요.

   B: 네. _____ 전화드릴게요. (도착하다)

–에 대해(서)

'–에 대해' is a short form of '–에 대하여' and is attached to a noun. It corresponds to 'about' in English. It is often followed by verbs like '알다', '모르다', '들어 보다', '설명하다', '이야기하다', '말하다', '관심이 많다', and etc.

–에 대해(서)
한국음식 : 한국 음식 + 에 대해서 → 한국 음식에 대해서 취미 : 취미 + 에 대해(서) → 취미에 대해(서)

저는 한국의 문화에 대해 관심이 많아요. I am very interested in Korean culture.

이 사원에 대해 들어 보셨을 거예요. I suspect you've heard about this temple.

이번 단체 여행에 대해 설명해드리겠습니다. Let me explain about this group trip.

☞ In addition to describe the subject of a sentence, '에 대해(서)' can also be used to describe an upcoming noun as an adjective, i.e. '–에 대한'.

이 책은 한국어 문법에 대한 책이에요. This book is about Korean grammar.

인터넷으로 날씨에 대한 뉴스를 확인해요.

I check the news about the weather on the Internet.

인스타그램에서 불고기 맛집에 대한 정보를 얻을 수 있어요.

You can get information about bulgogi restaurants on Instagram.

🍀 Create sentences using '에 대해' as in the example.

> **Ex** 다음 주 일정에 대해 이야기해요. (다음 주 / 일정 / 이야기하다)

(1) _____. (가이드/ 저 그림 / 설명하다)

(2) _____. (한국어 / 문법 / 질문하다)

(3) _____. (많은 사람들 / 건강 / 관심이 많다)

(4) _____. (내일 관광 / 계획 / 물어보다)

4 Response Exercise 응답 연습

Recommendation to tourist attraction 관광지 추천

Track 7-04

A 꼭 가봐야 할 관광지 좀 추천해 주세요.

Please recommend some tourist attractions we must visit.

[가 볼 만한 곳을 좀 추천해 주시겠어요?]

[Can you recommend some places worth visiting?]

B 백색사원과 코사무이섬을 추천합니다.
I recommend the White Temple and Ko Samui Island.

[백색사원과 코사무이섬에 한번 가 보세요.]
[Please go to White Temple and Ko Samui Island once.]

[백색사원과 코사무이섬은 꼭 봐야 할 곳이에요.]
[The White Temple and Ko Samui Island are must-see places.]

A 가장 가까운 관광지는 어디인가요? Where is the nearest tourist attraction?

[근처에서 어디를 관광하면 좋을까요?] [Where should I go sightseeing nearby?]

[어디를 방문하면 좋을까요?] [Where should I visit?]

B 국립박물관을 가 보세요. Please go to the National Museum.

Guide to arrival, departure, and announcement 도착과 출발, 공지 안내

Track 7-05

A 목적지에 도착했습니다. 이번 관광지는 치앙라이입니다. 저를 따라오세요.
We've arrived at our destination. The tourist attraction this time is Chiang Rai. Please follow me.

[제 깃발을 따라오세요, 제가 안내해 드릴게요.]
[Follow my flag, I'll show you around.]

[지금부터 저를 따라오세요. 이동하겠습니다.] [Follow me from now on, let's go.]

B 네, 알겠습니다. Yes, I see.

A 다 왔습니다. 여기에서 30분 정도 정차하겠습니다. 화장실 가실 분 계세요?
We're almost there. We'll stop here for about 30 minutes.
Is there anyone who wants to go to the restroom?

B 제가 차멀미하는 것 같아요. 약 좀 주세요.
I think I get carsick. Please give me some medicine.

A 지금부터 구경을 하시면 됩니다. 일행과 함께 다니세요.
You can look around from now on. Go with your party.

B 언제까지 돌아오면 돼요? When do I have to come back?

A 4시 전까지 버스로 돌아오세요. Come back to the bus before 4 o'clock.

A 점심 식사 장소입니다. 이곳에서 1시간 머물겠습니다.
This is the place for lunch. We'll stay here for an hour.

B 매운 음식을 주문하고 싶은데요. 얼마나 기다려야 하나요?
I'd like to order spicy food. How long do I have to wait?

Collection of travel information, and Inquiry about travel plans
여행 정보 수집, 계획 문의

Track 7-06

A 어떤 투어 상품들이 있나요? What kind of tour packages are there?
[관광 상품으로 어떤 것들이 있어요?] [What kind of tourist packages are there?]

B 반일 관광과 전일 관광이 있습니다. There are half-day tours and full-day tours.
[야간 투어도 있어요.] [There's also a night tour.]

A 가장 가까운 안내소가 어디예요? Where is the nearest information center?

B 시내 가는 길에 있습니다. It's on the way to the downtown.

A 어떤 관광을 하고 싶으세요? What kind of sightseeing do you want to do?

B 바닷가에 가고 싶은데요. I'd like to go to the beach.

A 어떤 종류 음식을 원하시나요? What kind of food do you want?

B 근처에 좋은 한식당으로 데려가 주세요.
Please take me to a good Korean restaurant nearby.

A 한국어가 가능한 가이드가 필요하신가요?
Do you need a guide who can speak Korean?

B 네, 한국인 가이드가 있으면 좋겠어요.
Yes, it would be good if we have a Korean guide.

Photography / Picture Taking 사진 촬영

A 어디에서 사진을 찍어야 제일 예뻐요?
Where should I take the most beautiful picture?

B 저기가 제일 잘 나와요. You can take the best over there.

A 저희들 사진 좀 찍어주세요. Please take a picture of us.
[준비됐어요. 찍으세요.] [We're ready. Please go ahead.]
[한 장 더 부탁합니다.] [One more, please.]

B 자, 찍습니다. 하나, 둘, 셋. Here we go. One, two, three.

A 같이 사진을 찍어도 돼요? Can I take a picture with you?
[셀카 같이 찍을까요?] [Shall we take a selfie together?]

B 물론이죠. 네, 좋습니다. Of course. Okay, good.
[죄송한데 전 사진 찍는 걸 싫어해요.] [Sorry, but I don't like to be taken pictures.]

A 폭포를 배경으로 찍어 주실 수 있어요?
Can you take a picture of the waterfall in the background?

B 그럼, 여기서 찍으면 안 예뻐요. Then, it's not pretty if you take it here.
[우측으로 조금만 가 주세요.] [Please go to the right a little bit.]
[한 발 뒤로 물러서 주세요.] [Please take a step back.]

Track 7-08

A 뭐가 제일 재미있었어요? What did you enjoy the most?

[뭐가 가장 좋았어요?] [What was your favorite?]

[어떤 점이 제일 좋았어요?] [What did you like the most?]

B 퀸스타운에서 해 본 번지점프가 너무 특별했어요.
The bungee jumping I've done in Queenstown was so special.

A 공연이 어떠셨어요? How was the performance?

B 마술쇼가 정말 멋졌어요. The magic show was amazing.

A 전통 마을에서 체험 잘 하셨어요?
Did you have a good experience in a traditional village?

B 네, 아주 특별한 체험이었어요. Yes, it was a very special experience.

5 Pronunciation 발음

Lateralization (유음화)

Track 7-09

When the final ㄹ is fronted by ㄴ and final ㄴ is fronted by ㄹ, we pronounce these as [ㄹ ㄹ]. In the above example, 'ㄴ' is pronounced as [ㄹ] when placed before or after 'ㄹ'. In the above example, when the final consonant 'ㄴ' in '연' is followed by the initial consonant 'ㄹ' in '락', it is pronounced [ㄹ]. Thus, '연락' is pronounced as [열락].

Ex 일년 → [일련]   한라산 → [할라산]   설날 → [설랄]   난로 → [날로]   편리 → [펼리]

A	■ 근처에서 가 볼 만한 관광지 좀 알려주세요.
	Please tell me some tourist attractions to visit nearby.
	■ 추천하실 만한 게 있나요? Do you have any recommendations?
B	어떤 것에 관심이 많으세요? What are you interested in?
	[어떤 것을 좋아하세요?] [What do you like?]
	[어떤 것을 추천해 드릴까요?] [What should I recommend?]
	[특별히 생각하고 있는 것이 있으세요?] [Do you have anything particular in mind?]

A	■ 저희들 사진 좀 찍어 주세요. Please take a picture of us.
	■ 이 휴대폰으로 사진 좀 찍어 주시겠어요?
	Can you take a picture with this phone?
	■ 한 장 더 찍어 주실 수 있나요? Can you take one more picture?
B	네, 한장 더 찍을게요. Yes, I'll take one more picture.

7　Culture of Korea

7.1　**When do Koreans travel abroad a lot?**
한국인이 해외여행을 많이 가는 시기

1) **Asia 1** (베트남 / 라오스 / 대만 / 발리 / 몽골)

	1	2	3	4	5	6	7	8	9	10	11	12
베트남 Vietnam	^_^		-▽-			⟩=⟨ Rainy Season					-▽-	^_^
	It's hot from May to October, but the high humidity leads to heavy rainfall.											

라오스 Laos	^_^				>=< Rainy Season						-▽-	^_^
Southeast monsoon brings 70% of annual rainfall and high humidity.												
대만 Taiwan	-▽-		^_^	>=< Rainy Season					-▽-		^_^	
Brutally hot and of high humidity in summer												
발리 Bali	>=<			-▽-			^_^		-▽-		>=<	
The island is subject to soupy, humid days throughout the year.												
몽골 Mongolia			>=<			^_^						
The summer season is characterized by sunny days and a little rain.												

^_^	Best	-▽-	OK	>=<	So so

2) Asia 2 (홍콩 / 필리핀 / 태국 / 코타키나발루 / 싱가포르)

	1	2	3	4	5	6	7	8	9	10	11	12
홍콩 Hong Kong	-▽-				>=< Rainy Season					^_^		
January–February is chilly in the morning and evening.												
필리핀 Philippines	^_^	-▽-				>=< Rainy Season						-▽-
A subtropical climate zone that can be divided into dry and rainy seasons												
태국 Thailand	-▽-		^_^			>=< Rainy Season				^_^	-▽-	
Hot and of humid in summer (Songkran in April/Loi Krathong in November)												
코타키나발루 Kota Kinabalu	>=<		-▽-			^_^		-▽-		>=<		
The island is subject to soupy, humid days throughout the year.												
싱가포르 Singapore	-▽-	^_^	^_^	^_^	-▽-							-▽-
December is the wettest month.												

^_^	Best	-▽-	OK	>=<	So so

3) Europe 1 (영국 / 스페인 / 독일 / 스위스 / 이탈리아 / 오스트리아 / 벨기에)

	1	2	3	4	5	6	7	8	9	10	11	12
영국 England							^_^					
	Many weekend street festivals are held in July to August.											
스페인 Spain	-▽-				^_^				^_^		-▽-	
	Good to travel throughout the year (Tomato Festival in August)											
독일 Germany					^_^		-▽-		^_^			
	Hot but not humid in July & August (Beer Festival in September & October)											
스위스 Switzerland	Ski Season				^_^							
	Good time: Zurich (May–June) & Interlaken (July–September)											
이탈리아 Italy					^_^				-▽-			
	High season of Rome is May to September (Venetian Carnival in February)											
오스트리아 Austria			-▽-		^_^		-▽-		^_^			
	Salzburg Music Festival in July & August											
벨기에 Belgium					-▽-			^_^	-▽-			
	EDM festivals in July/ Flower festivals in August											

^_^	Best	-▽-	OK	>=<	So so

4) Europe 2 (터키 / 프랑스 / 체코 / 헝가리 / 핀란드 / 크로아티아)

	1	2	3	4	5	6	7	8	9	10	11	12
터키 Turkey	>=<				^_^				^_^			>=<
	Good time: southern region (early summer)/all regions (Autumn)											
프랑스 France	>=<				^_^			-▽-			>=<	
	Quite cold in winter (Cannes Film Festival in May)											

	1	2	3	4	5	6	7	8	9	10	11	12
체코 Czech Republic				^_^				^_^				
	High Season is June to August. (Wine Festival in September to October)											
헝가리 Hungary	>=<			-▽-			^_^					>=<
	Its climate is very variable for short or extended periods.											
핀란드 Finland	Aurora Season				^_^						Aurora Season	
	The warmest weather in July and the coldest weather in February.											
크로아티아 Croatia	>=<			-▽-			^_^					>=<
	The weather varies greatly depending on the region.											

^_^	Best	-▽-	OK	>=<	So so

5) North America / Latin America (캐나다 / 하와이 / 브라질 / 페루 / 칠레)

	1	2	3	4	5	6	7	8	9	10	11	12
캐나다 Canada				^_^			-▽-		^_^			
	Climates vary by region. Four distinct seasons											
하와이 Hawaii					^_^		-▽-		^_^			
	Two seasons: Summer – May to October/ Winter – November to April											
브라질 Brazil	>=<				-▽-					-▽-		>=<
	Wild carnivals happening all over the country in February											
페루 Peru			>=<								>=<	
	Drier conditions along the southwest and wetter conditions along the east											
칠레 Chile	^_^										-▽-	^_^
	Mild summer – November to January. Wet winter – May to August											

^_^	Best	-▽-	OK	>=<	So so

6) Pacific Ocean (괌 / 사이판 / 몰디브 / 호주 / 뉴질랜드)

	1	2	3	4	5	6	7	8	9	10	11	12
괌 Guam	-▽-		^_^				>=<					-▽-
	Almost no change in temperature throughout the year											
사이판 Saipan	^_^		-▽-									-▽-
	Rainy season – May to October. Dry season – November to April.											
몰디브 Maldives	-▽-		^_^		>=<							-▽-
	Hot and humid tropical climate											
호주 Australia	>=<		-▽-						^_^		-▽-	>=<
	Four distinct seasons											
뉴질랜드 New Zealand	^_^		-▽-								-▽-	^_^
	The weather varies greatly by region. Mild climate throughout the year											

^_^	Best	-▽-	OK	>=<	So so

7.2 The recent trend of Koreans traveling abroad
한국인의 요즘 해외 여행 추세

1. **HASHTAGS** – Individualized and diversified travel preferences

2. **ANYONE** – A good trip with anyone

3. **BEYOND BOUNDARY** – Travel outside the box

4. **IN A WINK** – An impromptu trip that leaves right away when you want to leave

5. **THERAPY** – A healing trip that comforts and heals

6. **USUAL UNUSUAL** – An extraordinary daily life that has become a daily routine, and the trend of alternative travel continues

7. **SPECIAL ME** – Travel records that make 'my special moment'

8. **Filial trip** – A trip that can be remembered for a long time, feeling the togetherness and

unity of the family. Usually, children celebrate their parents' birthdays and anniversaries, and it could be gifting their parents to travel or they all go together with them.

9. **One Month Living Trip (Local Trip)** – It's not just a tourist attraction, but a trip to live like a local resident, discover something new in the area, and create your own travel destination.

10. **Barge Travel** – Originally, a barge means a ship that carries cargo or people when crossing a river. It refers to a combination of banana boats, water skis, and lake boards, which are common in vacation spots, and expresses a trip to enjoy exciting water sports after getting out of the boring water.

11. **Remind Travel** – A trip to visit the place you traveled in the past again and remember the pure and happy past and pledge your happy life and future ahead.

12. **Pool Villa Travel** – Accommodation with a swimming pool or hot spring in each room. You can eat your own meals and enjoy the ocean view in your personal space in the form of a balcony. It became popular as social distancing became common due to COVID-19.

7.3 Characteristics and Habits of Korean Tourists
한국 관광객들의 특징과 습관

1) Above all, the outstanding characteristic of Korean travelers is the phenomenon of "leaving a travel agency." Korean travelers prefer individual travel and use the "online reservation system" a lot to make cheap reservations for airlines and hotels.

2) Korean travelers value the use of the Internet. They check the availability of Wi-Fi in a hotel or restaurant.

3) Korean travelers always look for Asian food for one meal. No matter how well foreign food suits their taste, they usually eat at least one meal of Asian cuisine including Korean, Thai, Japanese, Vietnamese, and Chinese dishes.

4) Korean travelers' vacation period is short, so they try to see as much as possible in a limited time.

5) More and more travelers are using rental cars.

6) As various reviews of using the resort are being exposed through SNS, more and more customers want to pay attention to the details of the resort and enjoy it.

7) In general, group activities are preferred over personal time. There are many Korean travelers who like to take pictures, so they are eager to take pictures for personal SNS.

8) As the proportion of returning visitors increases, there is an increasing tendency to travel to areas with experience of visiting on topics other than for tourism purposes. It is a recent trend to travel like locals, such as healing, shopping, hot springs, and restaurants, as well as tourism in one area.

Answers

(1) A : 한국어 수업에 결석한 적이 있어요?

　　B : 네, 한국어 수업에 결석한 적이 있어요.

　　C : 아니요, 한국어 수업에 결석한 적이 없어요.

(2) A : 휴대 전화를 잃어버린 적이 있어요?

　　B : 네, 휴대 전화를 잃어버린 적이 있어요.

　　C : 아니요, 휴대 전화를 잃어버린 적이 없어요.

(3) A : BTS를 만난 적이 있어요?

　　B : 네, BTS를 만난 적이 있어요.

　　C : 아니요, BTS를 만난 적이 없어요.

(4) A : K-pop을 들은 적이 있어요?

　　B : 네, K-pop을 들은 적이 있어요.

　　C : 아니요, K-pop을 들은 적이 있어요.

(1) A : 불고기를 먹어 봤어요?

　　B : 네, 먹어 봤어요.

　　C : 아니요, 못 먹어 봤어요.

(2) A : 어릴 때 피아노를 배워 봤어요?

　　B : 네, 피아노를 배워 봤어요.

　　C : 아니요, 피아노를 못 배워봤어요.

(3) A : 유명한 운동 선수를 만나 봤어요?

　　B : 네, 만나 봤어요.

　　C : 아니요, 못 만나 봤어요.

(4) A : 바다에서 수영을 해 봤어요?

　　B : 네, 해 봤어요.

　　C : 아니요, 못 해 봤어요.

(1) A : 매운 음식을 먹을 수 있어요?　　(2) A : 한국어를 말할 수 있어요?

　　B : 네, 먹을 수 있어요.　　　　　　　　B : 아니요, 말할 수 없어요.

(3) A : 한복을 혼자 입을 수 있어요?　　(4) A : 오늘 저녁에 만날 수 있어요?

　　B : 아니요, 입을 수 없어요.　　　　　　B : 네, 만날 수 있어요.

Answers　　　　　　　　　　　　　　　　🖍 Dialogue 2

(1) 추천할 만해요.　(2) 볼 만해요.　(3) 먹을 만해요.　(4) 쇼핑할 만해요.

(1) 가장 좋아하는　(2) 가장 효과적인　(3) 가장 친한　(4) 가장 큰

(1) 방이 넓고 서비스가 좋아요.　　　　　(2) 피곤하고 졸려요.
(3) 빨래를 하고 집안 청소를 할 거예요.　(4) 맑고 더워요.

Answers　　　　　　　　　　　　　　　　🖍 Dialogue 3

(1) 점심을 먹은 후에 커피를 마십니다.　(2) 호텔에 체크인 한 후에 뭐 할 거예요?
(3) 계획을 세운 후에 여행을 하겠어요.　(4) 책을 읽은 후에 산책을 할 거예요.

(1) 설거지를 한 후에　　　　　　　　　　(2) 책을 다 읽은 후에
(3) 여권을 만든 후에　　　　　　　　　　(4) 도착한 후에

(1) 가이드가 저 그림에 대해 설명해요.
(2) 한국어 문법에 대해 질문해요.
(3) 많은 사람들이 건강에 대해 관심이 많아요.
(4) 내일 관광 계획에 대해 물어봐요.

8

천천히 보시고 필요한 게 있으면 말씀해 주세요

Take your time and let me know if you need anything

천천히 보시고 필요한 게 있으면 말씀해 주세요

Take your time and let me know if you need anything

1 Study Objectives 학습 목표

✎ To identify expressions related to shopping guide and sales (쇼핑 안내와 판매)

✎ To use expressions related to choosing, purchasing and checkout of the products (물건 고르기와 구매)

✎ To know expressions related to exchange and refund of the products (교환과 환불)

✎ To explain characteristics of the goods (물건 특징 설명하기)

2 Vocabulary 어휘

2.1 Dialogue Vocabulary 본문 어휘

Noun 명사 ✎

여름 summer	셔츠 shirt	흰색 white color
색상 color	제품 product	디자인 design
할인 discount	허리 waist	사이즈 size
바지 pants	환불 refund	교환 exchange
신상품 new product	수선 repair	카운터 / 계산대 counter

무료 for free   면세 tax free

Verb 동사 🖋

팔리다 be sold   고르다 choose   고치다 fix / mend

어울리다 suit

Others 나머지 🖋

짧다 short   날씬하다 slim   가능하다 It is possible

그냥 just   이상 above

마음에 들다 like a specific object or a person

2.2 Related Vocabulary 관련 어휘

상품 정보와 착용 안내 Merchandise Information and Wearing Guide 🖋

지갑 purse(F) / wallet(M)	원피스 dress	반바지 shorts
티셔츠 T-shirt	반팔 short-sleeve shirt	외투 overcoat
코트 coat	정장 suit	속옷 underwear
반지 ring	귀걸이 earring	목걸이 necklace
팔찌 bracelet	길다 long	작은 small
큰 large	중간 medium	아주 작은 extra small
아주 큰 extra large		

끼다 wear (장갑/반지)   쓰다 put on / wear (우산/모자/안경)

풀다 untie (넥타이/벨트/시계)   벗다 take off (옷/신발/배낭)

메다 shoulder (배낭)   매다 tie up (구두끈/넥타이)

들다 carry (핸드백)   차다 wear (시계/벨트/허리띠/팔찌)

빼다 take off / remove (반지/목걸이/귀걸이)　　　**신다** wear (구두/운동화/슬리퍼/샌들/양말)

하다 wear (귀걸이/넥타이/목걸이/목도리)

입다 put on (티셔츠/바지/원피스/외투/코트/반바지/정장/속옷)

쇼핑과 계산 Shopping and Checkout

가게 / 매장 store	쇼핑백 shopping bag	재고가 있는 in stock
매진 sold out	사다 buy	팔다 sell
주문하다 order	구매 purchase	판매 sale
쇼핑목록 shopping list	고객 customer	가격 price
특별가 special price	저렴한 cheap	비싼 expensive
바구니 basket	선반 shelf	가게 직원 shop assistant
가게 진열대 store shelves	재고 창고 stockroom	손수레 trolley
계산대 직원 cashier	현금 cash	잔돈 change
계산 checkout	불만 complaint	신용카드 credit card
줄 queue	영수증 receipt	쇼핑하러 가다 go shopping
비닐 봉지 plastic bag /carrier bag		

색깔 Color

하얀색 white	파란색 blue	회색 gray
까만색 black	분홍색 pink	노란색 yellow
주황색 orange	빨간색 red	남색 navy
갈색 brown	보라색 purple	초록색/녹색 green

3 Dialogue 대화

Dialogue 1 **Reception of visiting customers** 방문 고객 응대

Track 8-01

A 어서오세요?, 뭘 도와드릴까요? Hello? Can I help you?

B 괜찮아요. 그냥 구경하는 거예요. It's okay. I'm just looking around.

A 네, 천천히 보시고 필요한 게 있으면 말씀해 주세요.
Yes, take your time and let me know if you need anything.

B 네, 감사합니다. 제가 둘러 볼게요. Oh, thank you. I'll look around.

Key Grammar 핵심 문법

-고²

'-고' is used as a connective ending that attaches to verb stems to indicate the order of actions. It is also used to express that the action in the first clause was performed before the action in the second clause in chronological order. It corresponds to 'and (then)' in English.

−고²
손을 씻어요. + 저녁 식사를 해요. → 손을 씻고 저녁 식사를 해요. I wash my hands and then have dinner. 어제 저녁에 호텔에 체크인했어요. + 그리고 친구를 만났어요. → 어제 저녁에 호텔에 체크인하고 친구를 만났어요. I checked in at the hotel last night and then met my friend.

저는 아침을 먹고 공원에 가요. I eat breakfast and then go to the park.

저는 세수를 하고 이를 닦아요. I wash my face and then brush my teeth.

내 친구가 전화를 받고 나갔어요. My friend answered the phone and then left.

🍀 **Use the words in parentheses to complete the following sentences as in the example.**

Ex 표를 사고 영화를 봐요. (표를 사요, 영화를 봐요)

(1) _____ .
(숙제를 해요, 컴퓨터 게임을 해요)

(2) _____ .
(택시를 탔어요, 호텔에 갔어요)

(3) _____ .
(저녁에 부모님께 전화를 해요, 잠을 자요)

(4) _____ .
(오늘 오전에는 박물관에 가요, 오후에는 쇼핑할 거예요)

–(으)면

'–(으)면' is attached to a verb stem to express the meaning of once, if, when etc. in English.
When a verb stem ends with a vowel or a consonant 'ㄹ', '–면' is added.

When the verb stem ends with a vowel and a consonant ㄹ → '–면'	When the verb stem ends with a consonant → '–으면'
도착하다: 도착하 + 면 → 도착하면 살다: 살 + 면 → 살면	있다: 있 + 으면 → 있으면 입다: 입 + 으면 → 입으면

세부 공항에 도착하면 가이드가 나와있을 거예요.
There will be a guide when you arrive at Cebu Airport.

한국에 오랫동안 살면 한국어를 잘할 수 있어요.
If you live in Korea for a long time, you can speak Korean well.

시간 있으면 커피 한 잔 할까요?
If you have time, shall we have a cup of coffee?

♣ **Combine two sentences into one using '–(으)면' as in the example.**

Ex 좋은 사람이 있다 / 소개해 주다 → <u>좋은 사람이 있으면 소개해 줘요.</u>

(1) 주말에 시간이 많다 / 취미생활을 하다

→ _____ .

(2) K-pop을 듣다 / 기분이 좋아지다

→ _____ .

(3) 친구를 만나다 / 자주 노래방에 가다

→ ____.

(4) 날씨가 좋다 / 바다에 가다

→ ____.

Track 8-02

Dialogue 2 Product guidance and bargaining 제품 안내와 흥정

A 손님, 찾으시는 거 있으세요? Sir (Ma'am), are you looking for anything?

B 네, 여름에 입을 만한 셔츠를 찾고 있어요.
Yes, I'm looking for a shirt to wear in the summer.

A 어떤 색상을 찾으세요? 이 흰색 셔츠는 어떠세요?
What color are you looking for? How about this white shirt?

B 디자인은 마음에 드는데 좀 작은 것 같아요. 더 큰 사이즈는 없나요?
I like the design, but I think it's a little small. Do you have a bigger size?

A 죄송합니다만 이 사이즈만 남았네요. 다 팔렸어요.
I'm sorry, but we only have this size left. It's all sold out.

B 음, 이거 한번 입어 봐도 돼요? Well, can I try this on?

A 그럼요, 옷은 저쪽에서 갈아 입으시면 돼요. Of course, you can change over there.

아주 잘 어울리시네요. 흰색보다 빨간색 셔츠가 더 예뻐 보여요.

You look very good. The red shirt looks prettier than the white one.

B 이걸로 할게요. 좀 할인해 주시면 안 돼요?

I'll take this. Can you give me a discount?

A 셔츠 2개를 같이 사시면 400,000동에 드릴게요. 더 이상은 안 돼요.

If you buy two shirts together, I'll give you for 400,000 Dong. Not anymore.

Key Grammar 핵심 문법

-고 있다

'-고 있다' attaches to a verb stem to express an action in progress. When an action has started at some point in time and when he or she is still doing or continues the action, 'V-고 있다' can be used.

-고 있다
자다: 자 + 고 있다 → 자고 있다 먹다: 먹 + 고 있다 → 먹고 있다

아기가 지금 자고 있어요. A baby is sleeping right now.

호텔 식당에서 아침을 먹고 있어요. I'm having breakfast at the hotel restaurant.

지금 밖에 비가 오고 있어요. It's raining outside now.

♣ Complete the following sentences using '-고 있다' as in the example.

> **Ex** <u>누나가 거실에서 졸고 있어요.</u> (누나, 거실, 졸다)

(1) _____. (제임스 씨, 도서관, 책을 읽다)

(2) _____. (재민 씨, 미장원, 염색을 하다)

(3) _____. (동생, 거실, 텔레비전을 보다)

(4) _____. (친구, 커피숍, 기다리다)

-(으)ㄴ 것 같다 ◣

'-(으)ㄴ 것 같다' is attached to an adjective stem to express the speaker's conjecture regarding a state based on objective grounds. It corresponds to 'look like, sound like, appear that…' in English. It is also used to express the speaker's opinion or thought about something in a polite and gentle manner. It corresponds to 'I think…' in English. '- (으)ㄴ 것 같다' is used when speaker has a clear basis for the supposition, while '-(으)ㄹ 것 같다' is used when making a vague supposition.

When the adjective stem ends with a vowel a → '-ㄴ 것 같다'	When the adjective stem ends with a consonant → -은 것 같다
크다: 크 + ㄴ 것 같다 → 큰 것	짧다: 짧 + 은 것 같다 → 짧은 것 같다 작다: 작 + 은 것 같다 → 작은 것 같다

그 모자는 좀 큰 것 같아요.   I think that the hat is a little big.

이 치마는 너무 짧은 것 같아요. I think this skirt is too short.

이 호텔 방은 넓은 것 같아요. I think this hotel room is spacious.

🍀 **Use the expressions in parentheses to complete the following sentences as in the example.**

Ex 좀 비싼 것 같아요. (좀 비싸다)

(1) _____. (오늘 날씨가 좀 덥다)

(2) _____. (이 가방은 너무 작다)

(3) _____. (호텔 직원들이 바쁘다)

(4) _____. (공항에 사람들이 많다)

-네요

'-네요' is attached to the stem of a verb or an adjective to express the new fact that the speaker found out.

-네요
좋다: 좋 + 네요 → 좋네요
바쁘다: 바쁘 + 네요 → 바쁘네요

와! 경치가 좋네요. Wow! The scenery is nice.

A: 오늘은 점심 먹을 시간도 없어요. I don't even have time for lunch today.

B: 정말 바쁘네요. You are very busy.

공항에 늦게 도착해서 비행기를 놓쳤네요.

I missed my flight because I arrived at the airport late.

이 식당 음식이 정말 맛있네요. This restaurant's food is really delicious.

🍀 Complete the following sentences using '–네요' as in the example.

Ex 비가 오네요. (비, 오다)

(1) _____. (안나 씨, 한국어, 잘하다)

(2) _____. (이 호텔 숙박비, 너무 비싸다)

(3) _____. (퇴근 시간, 차, 막히다)

(4) _____. (이 커피, 정말, 맛있다)

Track 8-03

Dialogue 3 **Refund and Check out** 환불 및 계산

CASHIER

A 어서오세요. 뭘 사시겠어요? Welcome. What would you like to buy?

B 어제 산 옷인데 환불하고 싶어요.
I bought these clothes yesterday, but I want to return them to get a refund.

허리 사이즈에 비해 바지 길이가 좀 짧은 것 같아요.
I think the pants are a little short compared to the waist size.

A 죄송합니다만 환불은 안 됩니다. 대신에 교환은 가능합니다.
I'm sorry, but we don't give a refund. Instead, you can exchange it.

B 그러면 다른 바지로 고를게요. Then, I'll choose another pair of pants.

A 네, 그렇게 하십시오. 저쪽에 신상품도 많이 있는데 골라 보시겠어요?
Yes, go ahead. There are a lot of new products over there, so would you like to choose one?

B 이걸로 주세요. 이 바지가 어제 산 거보다 날씬해 보이네요. I'd like this one, please.
These pants look slimmer than what I bought yesterday.

혹시 길이 수선도 되나요? Can you fix the length?

A 네, 길이 수선은 무료로 해 드리고 있습니다. Yes, we offer free length repairs.

B 그거 잘 됐네요. 언제 찾을 수 있을까요? That's good. When can I get it?

A 내일 3시까지 고칠 수 있습니다. We can fix it by 3 o'clock tomorrow.

그래도 괜찮으시겠어요? Is that okay with you?

B 네, 좋아요. Yeah, that's great.

A 그럼, 계산은 카운터에서 도와드리겠습니다.
Well, I'll help you with the payment at the counter.

실례지만 영수증 좀 보여주세요. Excuse me, but can I see the receipt?

B 네, 여기요. 참, 면세로 살 수 있을까요?
Yes, right here. By the way, can I buy it at duty-free?

–에 비해(서)

'–에 비해(서)' is attached to a noun to draw comparisons within things. It is equivalent to saying "compared to N" in English. 'N에 비해' is similar to 'N보다' which means ".... than N".

–에 비해서
나이: 나이 + 에 비해(서) → 나이에 비해(서)   가격: 가격 + 에 비해(서) → 가격에 비해(서)

그는 나이에 비해(서) 아주 키가 큰 아이이다. He's a very tall child for his age.

지난번에 비해(서) 훨씬 더 쉽다. It's much easier now compared with last time.

시골은 도시에 비해(서) 공기가 좋아요.

Compared to city, the air in countryside is better.

작년에 비해(서) 올해 물건값이 많이 올랐어요.

Compared to last year, the price of goods has risen a lot this year.

🍀 **Complete the following sentences using** '–에 비해' **as in the example.**

Ex 이 컴퓨터가 그 컴퓨터에 비해 무거워요. (이 컴퓨터, 그 컴퓨터, 무겁다)

(1) _____. (망고, 딸기, 더 크다)

(2) _____. (한국사람들, 미국사람들, 성형수술, 많이 한다)

(3) _____. (7월 날씨, 6월 날씨, 더 더운 것 같다)

(4) _____. (이번 겨울, 작년, 더 추운 것 같다)

–보다

'–보다' attaches to a noun to compare two or more nouns. The sentences can be intensified with '더'. '보다' can be literally translated to 'in comparison to/than' and '더' as 'more' in English.

–보다
어제: 어제 + 보다 → 어제보다
겨울: 겨울 + 보다 → 겨울보다

어제보다 오늘이 더 더워요. It's hotter today than yesterday.

겨울보다 봄을 더 좋아해요? Do you like spring more than winter?

자카르타가 서울보다 더 복잡해요. Jakarta is more crowded than Seoul.

🍀 **Complete the following sentences using '–보다' as in the example.**

Ex <u>언니보다 내가 더 그림을 잘 그려요.</u> (언니, 내, 그림을 잘 그리다)

(1) _____. (서울, 델리, 복잡하다)

(2) _____. (형, 남동생, 키가 작다)

(3) _____. (한국어, 중국어, 어렵다)

(4) _____. (시장, 백화점, 비싸다)

–아어여 보이다

'어/아/여 보이다' is attached to an adjective stem to express an idea or feeling that is sub-jectively judged by looking at an object. It corresponds to 'It appears to be …' or 'It looks like …' in English.

When the adjective stem ends with a vowel a → '아 보이다'	When the adjective stem ends with a consonant → '어 보이다'	When the adjective stem ends with ending in –하다. → '해 보이다'
많다: 많 + 아 보이다 → 많아 보이다	젊다: 젊 + 어 보이다 → 젊어 보이다	피곤하다: 피곤 + 해 보이다 → 피곤해 보이다

좋은 차를 타고 다니는 웨이밍 씨는 돈이 많아 보여요.

Weiming who drives a nice car looks rich.

수민 씨는 나이가 많아도 젊어 보여요.

Soo-min looks young even though she is old.

제임스 씨는 일하고 있을 때 피곤해 보여요.

When James works, he looks tired.

🍀 **Complete the following sentences using** '–아/어/여 보이다' **as in the example.**

> **Ex** 안나 씨, 기분이 (좋다) <u>좋아 보여요.</u>

(1) 그 옷을 입으니까 조금 (뚱뚱하다) _____.

(2) 와, 케이크가 정말 (맛있다) _____!

(3) 원피스를 입으니까 아주 (예쁘다) _____.

(4) 저 반지가 (비싸다) _____.

Response to shoppers 쇼핑 고객 응대

Track 8-04

A 이걸로 할게요. I'll take this.

B 잘 어울리시네요. You look good.

[네, 딱 좋아요.] [Yes, it's perfect.]

[아주 좋아요. 손님께 잘 맞습니다.] [Very good. Good for you.]

[색상이 정말 잘 어울리세요.] [You look great in this color.]

A 이건 어때요? How about this?

B 잘 어울릴 것 같아요. I think it'll look good on you.

[네, 좋아 보이네요.] [Yes, it looks good.]

[손님께 잘 맞을 것 같아요.] [I think it'll fit well with you.]

[손님에게 잘 어울리지 않는 것 같아요.] [I don't think it suits you.]

A 이거 입어 봐도 돼요? Can I try this on?

B 네, 그러세요 Yes, go ahead.

[네, 물론입니다. 얼마든지요.] [Yes, of course. As much as you want.]

[그럼요, 탈의실은 저쪽입니다.] [Of course, the changing room is over there.]

A 무료 샘플 하나 주실 수 있어요? Can you give me a free sample?

B 공짜로 하나 가져 가세요. Please take one for free.

[가져 가세요. 그냥 나눠드리는 겁니다]. [Take it, please. we're just handing it out.]

Guide to inquiry about purchasing products 구입 제품 문의 안내

Track 8-05

A 어떤 스타일 신발을 찾으세요? What style of shoes are you looking for?

B 발이 편하고 가벼운 신발을 찾고 있어요.
I'm looking for shoes that are comfortable and light.

A 어떤 사이즈로 드릴까요? What size would you like?

B 스몰 사이즈로 주세요. I'd like a small size, please.
[라지 사이즈 입어요.] [I wear a large size.]

A 어떤 게 더 마음에 드세요? Which one do you like better?

B 결정을 못 하겠어요. 다른 것 좀 보여주세요.
I can't decide. Could you show me another one?

A 어떤 특산품을 사고 싶으세요? What kind of specialties do you want to buy?

B 가장 인기있는 제품으로 주세요. I'd like the most popular product, please.

Out of stock 품절

Track 8-06

A 파란색 모자로 교환하고 싶은데요. I'd like to exchange it for a blue hat.

B 죄송합니다만, 그건 다 나갔어요. I'm sorry, but it's all sold out.
[죄송하지만 그 제품은 다 나갔는데요.] [I'm sorry, but that products are all sold out.]
[죄송하지만 그 상품은 다 팔렸어요.] [I'm sorry, but the merchandise is sold out.]
[찾아봤는데 품절이네요.] [I looked it up and it's sold out.]

A 이 셔츠로 흰색이 있나요? Do you have this shirt in white?

B 죄송합니다만 그 상품이 이제 없습니다.
I'm sorry, but we don't have that product anymore.
[그 물품은 다 나갔습니다.] [That item is all gone.]
[지금 재고가 없습니다.] [We are out of stock right now.]

Haggling and selling 구매 흥정 및 판매

Track 8-07

A 너무 비싸요. 좀 할인 받을 수 있나요? It's too expensive. Can I get a discount?

[좀, 깎아줄 수 있어요?] [Could you please give me a discount?]

B 하나 사시면 하나를 더 드려요. If you buy one, I'll give you one more.

[하나 가격에 두 개 드립니다.] [We give you two for the price of one.]

[하나 사면 두 번째 상품은 50% 할인입니다.]

[If you buy one, you get 50% off for the second one.]

A 현금으로 계산하면 더 깎아 주실 수 있어요?

Can you give me a further discount if I pay in cash?

B 25달러에 드릴게요. 더 이상은 깎아 드릴 수 없어요.

I'll give it to you for $25. I can't give you any more discount.

[네, 그 가격에 맞춰 드릴게요.] [Yes, we'll match the price.]

[죄송하지만, 더는 안 됩니다.] [I'm sorry, but I can't do it anymore.]

[안 됩니다, 이미 할인된 금액입니다.] [No, it's already discounted.]

[안 돼요. 최대한 할인한 가격입니다.] [No way. It's a maximum discounted price.]

[그건 너무 밑지고 파는 거예요.] [we sell way at a loss.]

Packing request 포장 요청

Track 8-08

A 이거 선물용으로 포장해 주시겠어요? Can you wrap this up as a gift?

B 네, 포장은 유료입니다. 1개당 1달러씩 지불하셔야 합니다.

Yes, packaging would be charged. You have to pay a dollar for each.

[네, 예쁘게 포장해 드릴게요.] [Yes, I'll wrap it nicely for you.]

A 봉투에 같이 넣어 드릴까요? Do you want me to put it in a bag together?

B 아니요, 따로 담아 주세요. No, I'd like to have it separately.

A 쇼핑백에 넣어주세요. Please put it in the shopping bag.

B 네, 그러면 추가요금이 있습니다. Yes, then there would be an extra charge.

Pricing and payment methods 제품 계산 및 지불 방법

Track 8-09

A 계산은 어떻게 하시겠습니까? How would you like to pay?

[계산은 카운터에서 도와드리겠습니다.] [We'll help you pay at the counter.]

[현금이세요? 카드세요?] [Would it be cash or a card?]

[현금과 카드, 무엇으로 하시겠어요?] [Cash or card, what would you like?]

B 현금으로 계산하겠어요. I'll pay in cash.

[카드로 지불할게요.] [I'll pay by card.]

A 76달러예요. 신용카드, 아니면 현금? It's $76. Credit card or cash?

B 신용카드로 할게요. 여기요. I'll pay by a credit card. Here it is.

Duty free 듀티 프리

Track 8-10

A 면세 가격으로 살 수 있어요? Can I buy it at a duty-free price?

B 네, 여권 좀, 보여주세요. Yes, please show me your passport.

A 세금 환급 받으려면 어떻게 해야 되나요? How do I get a tax refund?

B 이 서류를 작성하시면 됩니다. What you need to do is to fill out this form.

[네, 환급 서류 준비해 드릴게요.] [Yes, we'll prepare the documents for the refund.]

A 이것을 교환하고 싶은데 큰 사이즈가 있나요?

I'd like to exchange this and do you have it in a big size?

B 아니요. 그건 사이즈가 따로 없습니다.

No. It doesn't come in a separate size.

A 이거 환불 받을 수 있을까요? Can I get a refund on this?

B 이 상품은 환불 불가 상품입니다. 뭐 때문에 그러시죠?

This product is non-refundable. What's wrong with it?

A 셔츠에 구멍이 있는데 새 것으로 교환할 수 있나요?

There is a hole in the shirt, can I exchange it for a new one?

B 네, 잠시만 기다려 주시겠어요? 불편하게 해 드려서 죄송합니다.

Yes, can you hold on a second? Sorry for the inconvenience.

A 어제 샀는데 작동을 안 해요. 환불받고 싶어요.

I bought it yesterday, but it doesn't work. I'd like a refund.

B 네, 해드릴게요. 결제하셨던 신용카드를 주시겠어요?

Yes, I will. Could you give me the credit card you used for payment?

A 이거 환불해 주세요. 아직 사용하지 않았어요.

Please give me a refund on this. I haven't used it yet.

B 영수증이 없으면 환불이 곤란합니다.

If you don't have a receipt, you can't get a refund.

Track 8-12

☑ **Palatalization** (구개음화)

When the final consonant ㄷ or ㅌ are followed by the vowel ㅣ, the ㄷ change to [ㅈ], and ㅌ change to [ㅊ], it is pronounced as [ㅌ] or [ㅊ]. But ㅌ followed by all other vowels retains it's own sound value*.

Ex 해돋이 [해도지]   같이 [가치]   끝이 [끄치]   붙이다 [부치다]   닫히다 [다치다]
   * 같아요 [가타요]

6 **Additional Expressions 추가표현**

A	■ 어서오세요. 좀 도와드릴까요? Welcome. Can I help you?
	┛ 특별히 찾으시는 거 있으세요? Are you looking for anything in particular?
	┛ 무엇을 찾으세요? What are you looking for?
	┛ 뭘 도와드릴까요? May I help you?

A	■ 어떤 것에 관심이 많으세요? What are you interested in?
	┛ 어떤 것을 좋아하세요? What do you like?
	┛ 어떤 것을 추천해 드릴까요? What would you like me to recommend?

7 Culture of Korea

7.1 Monetary Unit of Major Countries 주요 국가의 화폐 단위

나라 (country)	화폐 단위 (Monetary Unit)
한국 (South Korea)	원 (Won)
미국 (USA)	달러 (Dollar)
중국 (China)	위안 (Yuan)
일본 (Japan)	엔 (Yen)
러시아 (Russia)	루블 (Rouble)
대만 (Taiwan)	신 대만 달러 (New Taiwan dollar)
베트남 (Vietnam)	동 (Dong)
라오스 (Laos)	킵 (Kip)
태국 (Thailand)	밧 (Baht)
캄보디아 (Cambodia)	리엘 (Riel)
미얀마 (Myanmar)	짯 (Kyat)
말레이시아 (Malaysia)	링깃 (Ringgit)
싱가포르 (Singapore)	싱가포르 달러 (Singapore dollar)
필리핀 (Philippines)	페소 (Peso)
인도 (India)	루피 (Indian Rupee)
네팔 (Nepal)	루피 (Nepal Rupee)

7.2 Korean currency 한국의 화폐

The monetary unit of South Korea is 'won' and uses the symbol '₩'. Currently, four types of banknotes are in circulation in Korea. They are 50,000 won, 100,000 won, 5,000 won, and

1,000 won bills. The size of the bill gets bigger little by little as the amount goes up, so the 5,000 won note is slightly larger than the 1,000 won note, and the 10,000 won note is somewhat larger than the 5,000 won note. There are currently four types of coins in circulation: 10 won, 50 won, 100 won and 500 won coins.

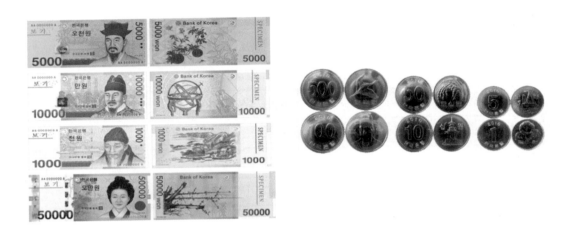

7.3 Shopping items that Koreans are interested in
한국인들이 관심 갖는 쇼핑 품목

1. Russia 러시아 – Matryoshka Dolls 마트료시카 인형, Carrot Cream 당근 크림, Beluga Vodka 벨루가 보드카, Alenka Chocolate 알료니카 초콜릿, Ushanka(fur hat) 털모자 우샨카, Shapka 샤프카

2. Australia 호주 – Manuka Honey 마누카꿀, Wool Products 양털제품과 의류, Eucalyptus Oil 유칼 립투스 오일, Lucas Papaw Cream 루카스포포 크림, Vegan Skincare 비건 스킨 케어제품

3. Germany 독일 – Ajona 아조나치약 Balea 발레아 화장품 Zwilling 헬켈 주방도구 Harib 하리보 젤리와 초콜릿 Kamill 카밀 립밤과 핸드크림 Rewe Bio 레베 바이오 건강제품

4. Japan 일본 – Mochi 모찌, Taiyaki 타이야키 과자, Kit Kat 킷캣 초콜릿, Shiseido 시세이도 SK-II 화장품, Arita 아리타 도자기류, Sony 소니 Canon 캐논 전자제품, Royce 로이스초콜릿, Rohto lycee 로토리세 안약과 인공눈물

5. Thailand 태국 – Yadom 야돔, Dried Fruits 말린 과일, Coconut Chips 코코넛 칩, Silk Scarf/

Pouch 실크 스카프/파우치, Pond's BB Powder 폰즈 BB 파우더

6. Taiwan 대만 – Taiwan Tea 타이완차, Nougat Cracker 누가크래커, Penglisu 펑리수, Bubble Tea Kits 버블티 키트, Yuki & Love 망고젤리, Darlie 달리 치약

7. Vietnam 베트남 – G7 Coffee G7 커피, Dried Fruits 말린 과일, Nuts 견과류, Mango Jelly 망고 젤리, Ratan Bag 라탄 가방, Noni Products 노니 제품

8. Hong Kong 홍콩 – Twinings Tea 트위닝스차, Chow Tai Fook 주타이푹 보석류, Jimmy Choo 지미츄 신발, Meadows milk tea 메도우 밀크티, Jenny Bakery Cookies 제니베이커리 쿠키, NinJion 닌지옴 목캔디

9. United States 미국 – Victoria's Secret Body Mist 빅토리아시크릿 바디미스트, Nutrition & Vitamins 영양제 & 비타민, Godiva Chocolate 고디바 초콜릿, Organic Cosmetics 오가닉 화장품, POLO, GAP Products POLO, GAP 제품, Starbucks Limited MD 스타벅스 한정 MD

10. Hawaii 하와이 – Coach/Toriburch Products 코치/토리버치 제품, Coffee Bean 커피 원두

11. Singapore 싱가포르 – Kaya Jam 카야잼, TWG Tea, Singapore Sling 싱가포르 슬링, Himalayan Lip Balm & Cream 히말라야 립밤 & 크림

12. France 프랑스 – bags 가방, wallets 지갑, accessories 액세서리, perfumes 향수, spices 향신료, cheese 치즈, wine 와인, tea 차, coffee 커피, chocolate 초콜릿, macarons 마카롱

13. Italy 이탈리아 – Raphael Chocolate 라파엘로 초콜릿, Pocket Coffee 포켓 커피, Mavis Toothpaste 마비스 치약, Santa Maria Novella Cosmetics 산타마리아노벨라 화장품, Pasta Noodles 파스타 면, Lemon Candy 레몬 사탕

14. Bali 발리 – Handcrafted rattan bag 수공예품 라탄백, beach supplies 비치용품, mosquito repellent 모기퇴치제, Bali coffee 발리 커피, woodcraft 목공예품, wooden cutting board 나무 도마

15. Kota Kinabalu 코타키나발루 – Coconut white coffee 코코넛 화이트커피, anchovy snack 멸치 과자, Saba traditional tea 전통차, goat milk cream 산양유 크림

Answers

(1) 숙제를 하고 컴퓨터 게임을 해요.

(2) 택시를 타고 호텔에 갔어요.

(3) 저녁에 부모님께 전화를 하고 잠을 자요.

(4) 오늘 오전에는 박물관에 가고 오후에는 쇼핑할 거예요.

(1) 주말에 시간이 많으면 취미생활을 해요.

(2) K-pop을 들으면 기분이 좋아져요.

(3) 친구를 만나면 자주 노래방에 가요.

(4) 날씨가 좋으면 바다에 가요.

Answers

(1) 비빔밥이 맛있어요.   (2) 자동차가 많아요.

(3) 지하철이 빨라요.   (4) 제임스씨가 밥을 먹어요.

(1) 택시로 갈 거예요.   (2) 현금으로 지불하겠어요.

(3) 젓가락으로 먹어요.   (4) 유트브로 공부해요.

(1) 아침에 운동을 하겠습니다.   (2) 저는 비빔밥을 먹겠습니다.

(3) 제가 커피를 사 오겠습니다.   (4) 예약을 확인해 드리겠습니다.

(1) 망고가 딸기에 비해서 더 커요.

(2) 한국 사람들이 미국 사람들에 비해서 성형수술을 많이 해요.

(3) 7월 날씨가 6월 날씨에 비해서 더 더운 것 같아요.

(4) 이번 겨울이 작년 겨울에 비해서 더 추운 것 같아요.

(1) 서울보다 델리가 복잡해요.　　　　(2) 형이 남동생보다 키가 작아요.

(3) 한국어보다 중국어가 어려워요.　　　(4) 시장보다 백화점이 비싸요.

(1) 뚱뚱해 보여요.　(2) 맛있어 보여요.　(3) 예뻐 보여요.　(4) 비싸 보여요.

9

곧 다른 버스를 대절하도록 하겠습니다
We'll rent another bus soon

Unit 9

곧 다른 버스를 대절하도록 하겠습니다

We'll rent another bus soon

---

1 **Study Objectives** 학습 목표

✎ To resolve unexpected situations such as accidents
  (사고와 같은 돌발상황 해결)

✎ To respond to emergencies such as theft or loss
  (도난, 분실과 같은 비상상황 대처)

✎ To notify emergency situations such as illness or injury
  (질병, 부상과 같은 응급 상황 지원 요청)

---

2 **Vocabulary** 어휘

2.1 **Dialogue Vocabulary** 본문 어휘

Noun 명사 ✎

접촉 사고 collision accident	상황 situation	지갑 wallet
도난 신고(서) theft report	축구 soccer	경기 game
출구 exit	지퍼 zipper	열 fever
이틀 two days	진통제 painkiller	두통 head ache
감기 cold	증상 symptom	처방전 prescription
컨디션 condition	약 medicine	

Verb 동사 🖊

다치다 get hurt

놀라다 be surprised

대절하다 rent

작성하다 write

돕다 help

주무시다 sleep (honorific)

Others 나머지 🖊

가볍다 light

하마터면 almost

편찮으시다 sick (honorific)

정신이 없다 out of one's mind

일단 once

2.2 Related Vocabulary 관련 어휘

교통사고와 응급상황 Traffic Accident and Emergency Situation 🖊

보행자 pedestrian

차에 치이다 be hit by a car

안정시키다 set at ease

추돌하다 run into

상황을 파악하다 grasp the situation

뺑소니 hit and run

속도 제한 speed limit

부딪히다 be bumped into

전복 사고 overturning accident

응급상황을 처리하다 handle the first aid

정면 충돌 head-on collision

차량 vehicle

다투다 quarrel

의약품 Pharmaceutical Products 🖊

거즈 gauze

감기약 cold medicine

멀미약 nausea medicine

해열제 fever reducer

두통약 headache pill

인공누액 artificial tears

파스 pain relief patch

소독약 disinfectant

소화제 digestive pills

변비약 laxative

진통제 painkiller

영양제 supplement

수면제 sleeping pills

상처보호연고 wound protection ointment

밴드 bandage

위염약 gastritis medicine

지사제 diarrhea medicine

소염제 anti-inflammatory

화상연고 burn ointment

진정제 sedative

부상과 치료 Injury and Treatment ✏️

주사를 맞다 have an injection　　링거를 맞다 get an IV　　물에 빠지다 fall into the water

약을 먹다 take medicine　　넘어지다 fall down　　바르다 apply

붙이다 stick　　넣다 put in　　뿌리다 spread

접지르다 sprain　　움직이지 않게 하다 jam

체온을 재다 take one's temperature　　계단에서 구르다 roll on the stairs

붕대를 감다 put a bandage around

증상 Symptom ✏️

소화가 안 되다 have indigestion　　콧물이 나오다 have a runny nose

기침을 하다 cough　　재채기가 나다 sneeze

머리가 아프다 have a headache　　열이 나다 have a fever

체하다 have a digestive upset　　피부가 가렵다 one's skin itches

다리를 다치다 hurt one's leg　　코가 막히다 have a stuffy nose

목이 붓다 have a swollen throat　　배가 아프다 have a stomachache

눈병이 나다 have an eye disease　　배탈이 나다 have an upset stomach

설사를 하다 have diarrhea　　발목을 삐다 sprain one's ankle

Dialogue 1 **Accident** 사고

Track 9-01

끼익!!!! ~ Squeak!

A 죄송합니다. 모두 괜찮으세요? I'm sorry. Is everyone all right?

다친 분이 계신가요? Is anyone hurt?

B 어머, 무슨 일이에요? Oh, what's going on?

A 앞 차하고 가벼운 접촉사고가 난 것 같습니다.
I think there was a minor collision with the car in front of us.

일단 버스에서 내려 주세요. Please get off the bus for now.

상황을 확인 후 곧 다른 버스를 대절하도록 하겠습니다.
I'll check the situation and rent another bus soon.

정말 죄송합니다. I'm so sorry.

B 다행이에요. 하마터면 큰일날 뻔했네요. That's a relief. That was close.

-도록

'-도록' is attached to verbs and adjectives to indicate the purpose, result, degree, or method of the situation that follows..

-도록
지나가다 + 도록 → 지나가도록 늦지 않다 + 도록 → 늦지 않도록

1: It is attached to stems of verbs and some adjectives to indicate the purpose or standard for the actions that follow.

사람들이 지나가도록 우리들은 비켜섰다. We stood aside for the people to pass by.

다음에는 절대 늦지 않도록 조심하세요. Be careful not to be late next time.

여행지에서 다치지 않도록 조심하세요.

Be careful not to get hurt at the travel destination.

2: It is attached to a verb stem and indicates the method and degree of action that follows.

그는 몸살이 나도록 열심히 일했다. He worked hard to get sick.

학생들이 목이 터지도록 응원했습니다.

The students cheered until they're heard screaming.

우리는 발이 아프도록 걸어 다녔어요. We walked around until our feet hurt.

3: It is attached to the verb stem and indicates the limit of time.

내 동생이 12시가 다 되도록 아직 집에 안 들어왔어요.

My brother hasn't come home yet until it's almost 12 o'clock.

한 달이 넘도록 전화 한 통이 없어요. I haven't had a phone call in over a month.

손님 한 분이 출발할 때가 다 되도록 아직 버스에 돌아오지 않았어요.

A customer hasn't come back to the bus yet when it's almost time to leave.

🍀 **Combine two sentences into one using '-도록' as in the example.**

> **Ex** 공항에 늦지 않다 / 일찍 서두르세요.
> → <u>공항에 늦지 않도록 일찍 서두르세요.</u>

(1) 손님들이 편히 쉬다 / 조용히 했다

　→ _____ .

(2) 감기에 걸리지 않다 / 손을 잘 씻어야겠네요.

　→ _____ .

(3) 교환하지 않다 / 옷을 입어보고 샀다

　→ _____ .

(4) 밤이 새다 / 이야기를 했다

　→ _____ .

−(으)ㄹ 뻔하다　　　　　　　　　　　　　　　　　　　　　　　　▶

'−(으)ㄹ 뻔하다' is attached to a verb stem to indicate something almost happened but did not. It is often used together with adverb 하마터면 (almost, nearly) to emphasize the near occurrence of an event that could have happened. It is also used to exaggerate what the situation was in the past.

When the verb stem ends with a vowel and a consonant ㄹ → '-ㄹ 뻔하다'	When the verb stem ends with a consonant → '-을 뻔하다'
놓치다: 놓치 + ㄹ 뻔하다 → 놓칠 뻔하다 울다: 우 + ㄹ 뻔하다 → 울 뻔하다	죽다: 죽 + 을 뻔하다 → 죽을 뻔하다 늦다: 늦 + 을 뻔하다 → 늦을 뻔하다

하마터면 비행기를 놓칠 뻔했어요. We almost missed the flight.

영화가 너무 슬퍼서 하마터면 여자 친구 앞에서 울 뻔했어요.

The movie was so sad I almost cried in front of my girlfriend.

배가 너무 고파서 죽을 뻔했어요. I was very hungry (that I almost die).

🍀 **Change the following sentences to have the same meaning using '-(으)ㄹ 뻔하다' as in the example.**

Ex 일요일에 오지 않아서 구경을 할 수 있었어요.
→ 일요일에 왔더라면 구경을 못 할 뻔했어요.

(1) 길이 안 막혀서 비행기를 놓치지 않았어요.

→ _____.

(2) 아침에 일찍 일어나서 약속을 지킬 수 있었어요.

→ _____.

(3) 신용카드가 있어서 지하철을 탈 수 있었어요.

→ _____.

(4) 공부를 열심히 해서 대학교에 합격을 할 수 있었어요.

→ _____.

A 도와주세요. Please help me.

B 어떻게 도와드릴까요? How can I help you?

A 지갑을 잃어버렸어요. 도난 신고를 하고 싶어요.
I lost my wallet. I want to report a theft.

B 언제요? 어떤 일이 있으셨나요? When? What happened?

A 축구경기를 보고 왔는데 그때 같아요.
I watched a soccer game and went out. It seems to happen at that time.

나올 때 출구에 사람들이 많아서 정신이 없었어요.
There were a lot of people at the exit when I went out, so I was out of it.

B 많이 놀라셨겠어요. You must have been very surprised.

어떤 지갑이에요? 무엇이 들어있었나요?
What kind of wallet is it? What was in it?

A 지퍼가 달린 검은색 지갑이에요. It's a black wallet with a zipper.

카드가 들어 있어서 가방 안에 넣고 다녔어요.
There was a card in the bag, so I carried it around.

B 빨리 찾을 수 있도록 도와드리겠습니다. I'll help you so that you can find it quickly.

먼저 도난신고서 좀 작성해 주세요. Please fill out the theft report first.

A 여기요. 찾으면 여기로 전화해 주세요. Here it is. If you find it, please call me here.

B 네, 지갑을 찾게 되면 바로 연락 드리도록 하겠습니다.
Yes, I'll contact you as soon as I find your wallet.

Key Grammar 핵심 문법

-아/어/여 버리다

It is used to express speaker's feeling to the completed event/action (that nothing remained after completion), i.e. a happy feeling about finally completing a task and getting rid of a burden, or a sad feeling that something completed in an unexpected way.

Since the expression can indicate various emotional states, it is important to understand the emotional state of speaker from the particular context (e.g. happy or sad).

When a verb stems ending in the vowels ㅏ or ㅗ. → '-아 버리다'	When a verb stems ending in other vowels. → '-어 버리다'	When a verb stems ending in -하다. → '해 버리다'.
가다: 가 + 아 버리다 → 가 버리다	먹다: 먹 + 어 버리다 → 먹어 버리다	시작하다: 시작 + 해 버리다 → 시작해 버리다

10분밖에 안 늦었는데 친구는 저를 기다리지 않고 가 버렸어요.

Although I was late for 10 minutes only, my friend left without waiting.

그 영화가 벌써 시작해 버렸어요. That movie is already ended. (So, I am sad.)

내가 사다 놓은 케이크를 동생이 다 먹어 버렸어요.

My little brother ate all the cake that I bought.

🍀 **Complete the following sentences using '–아어여 버리다' as in the example.**

> **Ex** 오늘 아침에 우리는 남은 음식을 다 <u>먹어 버렸어요</u>. (먹다)

(1) 제임스 씨가 늦게 와서 음식이 다 _____. (식다)

(2) 안나 씨는 눈물을 참다가 결국 _____. (울다)

(3) 내가 공항에 도착했을 때 비행기는 이미 _____. (출발하다)

(4) 어제 나는 동생에게 있는 돈을 다_____. (주다)

–(으)ㄹ 때 ◥

It is attached to the stem of a verb or an adjective to express the time an action or state occurs, has happened or will take place.

When the verb or an adjective stem ends with a vowel and a consonant ㄹ → '–ㄹ 때'	When the verb or an adjective stem ends with a consonant → '–을 때'
다니다: 다니 + ㄹ 때 → 다닐 때 피곤하다: 피곤하 + ㄹ 때 → 피곤할 때	먹다: 먹 + 을 때 → 먹을 때 씻다: 씻 + 을 때 → 씻을 때

대학교에 다닐 때 스페인어를 배웠어요. I learned Spanish when I was in college.

피곤할 때는 쉬는 게 좋아요. It's good to rest when you're tired.

점심을 먹을 때 친구가 찾아왔어요.
A friend of mine came to see me when I was having lunch.

♣ Complete the following sentences as in the example.

> **Ex** 여권을 <u>만들 때</u> 사진이 필요해요. (만들다)

(1) 부모님이 _____ 부모님께 전화를 해요. (보고 싶다)

(2) 밥을 _____ 소리를 내지 마세요. (먹다)

(3) 저는 기분이 _____ 음악을 들어요. (나쁘다)

(4) 집에 _____ 아무도 없었어요. (도착했다)

-아서/어서/여서 (reason)[2]

This pattern is used to connect the second clause to the first to express a cause or reason. It corresponds to 'because (of)' in English.

When a verb stems or an adjective ending in the vowels ㅏ or ㅗ. → '-아서'	When a verb or an adjective stems ending in other vowels. → '-어서'	When a verb or an adjective stems ending in -하다. → '-해서'.
만나다: 만나 + 아서 → 만나서 오다: 오 + 아서 → 와서	막히다: 막히 + 어서 → 막혀서 예쁘다: 예쁘 + 어서 → 예뻐서	운동하다: 운동 + 해서 → 운동해서 심심하다: 심심 + 해서 → 심심해서

여러분, 만나서 반가워요. Nice to meet you, everyone.

눈이 와서 길이 미끄러워요. The road is slippery because of the snow.

길이 막혀서 늦었어요. I was late because there was a traffic jam.

그 여자가 너무 예뻐서 저는 그녀를 만나고 싶어요.

She's so pretty that I want to meet her.

운동해서 땀이 많이 나요. I sweat a lot because I worked out.

심심해서 친구에게 전화했어요. I called my friend because I was bored.

☞ Because the particles that represent tense such as '-었-' or '-겠-' cannot be combined with '-아/어/여서', the tense of such sentences is expressed in the second clause.

밥을 많이 먹었어서 배가 불러요. (x)

밥을 많이 먹어서 배가 불러요. (O) I'm stuffed because I ate a lot.

이 식당은 음식이 맛있겠어서 사람이 많아요. (x)

이 식당은 음식이 맛있어서 사람이 많아요. (O)

This restaurant is crowded because the food is delicious.

☞ This pattern cannot be used in sentences ending with '-세요', '-(으)ㄹ까요?', or '-(으)ㅂ시다'.

길이 막혀서 지하철을 타세요. (x)

길이 막혀서 지하철을 탑시다. (x)

길이 막혀서 지하철을 탈까요? (x)

길이 막히니까 지하철을 타세요. (O) Take the subway because there's traffic.

🍀 **Use the expressions in parentheses to complete the following sentences as in the example.**

Ex 머리가 아파서 회사에 못 갔어요. (머리가 아프다 / 회사에 못 갔다)

(1) _____. (일이 많다 / 집에 못 가다)

(2) _____. (길이 좁다 / 차가 지나갈 수 없다)

(3) _____. (눈이 많이 내리다 / 비행기가 연착되었다)

(4) _____. (옷이 작다 / 입기가 어렵다)

Track 9-03

Dialogue 3 **Injuries, When you're sick** 부상과 질병

A 저기요, 제가 아파요. Excuse me, I'm sick.

B 어디가 편찮으세요? Where does it hurt?

지금 증상은 어떠세요?

What are your symptoms now?

A 열이 나고 머리가 아파요. I have a fever and a headache.

약을 먹었는데 낫지 않아요. I took medicine, but it doesn't get better.

B 언제부터 그랬어요? Since when?

A 아픈 지 이틀 정도 됐어요. I've been sick for about two days.

약도 먹고 쉬었는데 나아지지 않네요.

I took medicine and rested, but it doesn't get better.

B 감기인 것 같은데, 다른 증상은 없으세요?

I think it's a cold, do you have any other symptoms?

A 목도 좀 아파요. My throat hurts a little, too.

처방전 없이 약을 살 수 있을까요? Can I buy medicine over the counter?

B 네, 마트에서 간단한 약은 살 수 있어요. Yes, you can buy simple medicine at the mart.

우선 제가 가지고 있는 약을 드릴게요. First, I'll give you the medicine I have.

여기 약이 있습니다. Here's the medicine.

A 어머, 고맙습니다. Oh, thank you.

이 약을 언제 먹으면 되나요? When should I take this medicine?

B 식사하시고 나서 30분 뒤에 드세요. Please take it 30 minutes after the meal.

주무시고 나면 컨디션이 좋아질 거예요. You'll feel better after you sleep.

A 네, 고맙습니다. Yes, thank you.

Key Grammar 핵심 문법

–(으)ㄴ 지

'–(으)ㄴ 지' attaches after a verb stem. '은/ㄴ' is an ending of a word that makes the preceding word function as an adnominal phrase and indicates an event or action that has occurred in the past. '지' is a bound noun used to indicate that a certain time has passed since a certain act mentioned in the preceding statement is done. It is followed by verbs indicating the passage of time, such as '되다 (become), 지나다 (pass), 넘다 (exceed), 흐르다 (pass), 경과하다 (pass).' Those verbs are usually used 'past tense' as it is usually used to mean that time has already passed.

When the verb stem ends with a vowel and a consonant ㄹ → '-ㄴ 지'	When the verb stem ends with a consonant → '-은 지'
오다: 오 + ㄴ 지 → 온 지 살다: 사 + ㄴ 지 → 산 지	먹다: 먹 + 은 지 → 먹은 지 앉다: 앉 + 은 지 → 앉은 지

비가 온 지 한 달이 됐어요. It has been a month since it rained.

서울에 산 지 이제 두 달 됐어요. It has been now two months since I lived in Seoul.

점심을 먹은 지 한 시간이 지났어요. It's been an hour since I had lunch.

🍀 **Use the expressions in parentheses to complete the following sentences as in the example.**

Ex (안나 씨가 집에 가다 / 한 시간이 넘었는데요)
→ 안나 씨가 집에 간 지 한 시간이 넘었는데요.

(1) (담배를 끊다 / 세 달이 지났어요) → _____.

(2) (휴대폰을 사다/ 하루 만에 고장이 났어요) → _____.

(3) (한국어를 공부하다 / 2년이 됐어요) → _____.

(4) (그 책을 읽다 / 오래돼서 내용이 잘 기억나지 않아요)

→ _____.

-고 나서

'-고 나서' is attached to a verb stem to indicate that an action is completed and then another action or a situation occurs.

−고 나서
내리다: 내리 + 고 나서 → 내리고 나서
씻다: 씻 + 고 나서 → 씻고 나서

버스에서 사람들이 다 내리고 나서 타야 해요.

You have to get on after everyone gets off the bus.

손을 씻고 나서 밥을 먹어요. I eat after washing my hands.

비가 오고 나서 날씨가 갑자기 추워졌어요.

The weather suddenly got cold after the rain.

🍀 **Complete the following sentences using '−고 나서' as in the example.**

Ex 열심히 공부하고 나서 시험을 봐요. (열심히 공부하다, 시험을 봐요)

(1) _____. (공연이 끝나다, 식당에 갈 거예요)

(2) _____. (책을 다 읽다, 잠을 잤어요)

(3) _____. (설거지를 하다, 빨래를 했어요)

(4) _____. (친구가 가다, 갑자기 외로워졌다)

−아/어/여지다

1. It is attached to the verb stem to indicate that subject's action or behavior occurs either because of an action performed by someone else or because of some other indirect action performed by some person or thing or that an action occurs on its own and becomes such a state.

2. It's attached to an adjective, indicating that it's gradually becoming a certain state.

When a verb stems or an adjective ending in the vowels ㅏ or ㅗ. → '-아지다'	When a verb or an adjective stems endingin other vowels. → '-어지다'	When a verb or an adjective stems ending in -하다. → '-해지다'.
쏟다: 쏟 + 아지다 → 쏟아지다	켜다: 켜 + 어지다 → 켜지다 ('어' is redundant so it is dropped.)	정하다: 정+ 해지다 → 정해지다

커피가 쏟아져서 옷에 얼룩이 생겼어요.

The coffee was spilled and I have a stain on my clothes.

휴대전화가 안 켜져요. My cell phone won't turn on.

일정이 정해지면 알려주세요. Please let me know when the schedule is decided.

♣ **Complete the following sentences using** '-아/어/여지다' **as in the example.**

Ex 등산로 입구를 지나면 길이 이 두 개로 <u>나누어져요</u>. (나누다)

(1) 그 사람을 만나면 마음이 _____ . (편하다)

(2) 엘리베이터 안에서 전화가 _____ . (끊다)

(3) 직장을 그만두고 싶지만 _____ . (망설이다)

(4) 날씨가 너무 추우니까 봄이 _____ . (기다리다)

Response to an unexpected situation & traffic accidents
사고, 돌발 상황 응대

Track 9-04

A   6번 국도에서 교통 사고가 났어요.   There was a traffic accident on Route 6.

제가 차에 치었어요.   I was hit by a car.

B   앰뷸런스를 부를까요?   Should I call an ambulance?

A   제 아이가 없어졌어요. 방송을 해 주세요.

My child is missing. Please do the broadcast.

B   네, 지금 방송 안내하겠습니다. 자녀분 인상착의가 어떻게 되지요?   Yes, I'll announce
the broadcast now. What's your child's description?

A   한국어 통역하시는 분 안 계세요? 급해요.

Is there anyone who can translate Korean? It's urgent.

B   잠시만요. 바로 찾아 보겠습니다.   Wait a minute. I'll look for it right away.

A   도움이 필요합니다. 어서 도와 주세요.   I need your help. Please help me right away.

B   괜찮으세요? 의식 잃지 마세요. 지금 곧 가까운 병원으로 가겠습니다.

Are you okay? Don't lose your consciousness. We'll take you to the nearest hospital
soon.

[괜찮으세요? 지금 곧 응급구조센터에 연락하겠습니다.]

[Are you okay? I'll call the emergency services right now.]

A   이런 경우에 어떻게 해요? 한국 영사관에 전화 좀 해 주세요.

What do you do in this case? Please call the Korean consulate.

B   네, 한국 영사관에 전화해서 알아 보겠습니다.

Yes, I'll call the Korean consulate and find out.

Responding to reports of lost 도난, 분실물 신고 응대

A 관광지는 소매치기가 많은 곳입니다. 항상 조심하세요.
There are a lot of pickpockets in the tourist attractions. Be careful all the time.

B 네, 명심할게요. Yes, I'll keep that in mind.

A 휴대전화기를 잃어 버렸어요. I lost my cellphone.

B 언제 분실하신 것 같아요? 가방이나 호텔 방도 찾아보셨어요?
When do you think you lost it? Have you looked for a bag or a hotel room, too?

A 제 휴대폰을 찾을 방법이 없을까요? Is there any way I can find my cellphone?

B 경찰서에 가서 도난 신고를 하세요. Go to the police station and report the theft.

A 호텔 방 카드키를 잃어 버렸어요. 조금 전까지 있었는데요.
I lost my hotel room card key. It was with me a while ago.

B 어디에 두셨나요? 더 찾아볼까요? Where did you put it? Shall I look for more?

A 방을 비운 사이에 귀중품을 도둑맞았어요.
My valuables were stolen while I was away from my room.

B 일단 호텔 카운터에 문의해 보세요. Please contact the hotel counter for now.

A 신용카드를 잃어버렸어요. I lost my credit card.

B 먼저 분실신고를 하시고 신용카드를 정지시켜야 됩니다.
You have to report the loss first and then block your credit card.

[카드 재발행을 도와드릴까요?] [May I help you reissue your card?]

A 여권을 찾을 수가 없어요. I can't find my passport.

B 마지막으로 본 게 언제인지 기억나세요?
Do you remember when you last saw it?

우선 한국 대사관에 연락을 해야 해요.
First of all, you have to contact the Korean Embassy.

A 여권을 분실했습니다. 재발급 받을 수 있나요?
I lost my passport. Can I get it reissued?

B 네, 하지만 한국 영사관에 가셔야 합니다.
Yes, but you need to go to the Korean consulate.

A 지갑을 소매치기 당했어요. My wallet was pickpocketed.

B 근처 경찰서에 연락해 보세요. Please contact nearest police station.

A 가방을 도둑맞았어요. 어떻게 해야 하나요? My bag was stolen. What should I do?

B 얼마가 들어있었나요? How much was in it?

[찾으면 전화할게요.] [We'll call you if we find it.]

[이 양식을 작성해 주시겠어요?] [Could you fill out this form?]

A 택시에 가방을 두고 내렸어요. I left my bag in the taxi.

B 한국 대사관에 연락해 보세요. Please contact the Korean Embassy.

A 짐이 보이지 않아요. 제 짐을 잃어버린 것 같아요.
I can't see my luggage. I think I lost my luggage.

B 어디에 짐을 놓으셨어요? 프론트에 맡기셨나요?
Where did you put your luggage? Did you leave it at the front desk?

[마지막으로 짐을 두신 곳이 어디세요? 프론트에 맡기셨어요?]
[Where was the last place you left your luggage? Did you leave it at the front desk?]

A 분실물 센터는 어디에 있어요? Where is the Lost and Found?

B 제 1 여객터미널 지하 1층에 있어요. It's on B1 of Passenger Terminal 1.

A 이 근처에 분실물 센터가 있나요? Is there a Lost and Found near here?

B 이 근처에는 없고 가까운 경찰서에 가서 접수하세요.
There isn't one around here, so go to the nearest police station.

A 제 짐을 찾을 수 없습니다. I can't find my baggage.

B 여행 가방의 브랜드 이름을 기억하세요?
Do you remember the brand name of your suitcase?

거기에 특별한 표시가 있나요? Are there any special marks on it?

A 제 짐을 찾을 가능성이 있나요? Are there any chances of locating my baggage?

B 걱정하지 마세요. 손님의 여행 가방을 찾기 위해 모든 노력을 다하겠습니다.
Don't worry. We'll make every effort to locate your suitcase.

Response to illness/injury and emergency 질병과 부상, 응급상황 응대

Track 9-06

A 의사를 불러 주세요. Please call a doctor.

[저를 병원으로 데려다 주세요.] [Take me to a hospital, please.]

[구급차를 불러 주세요.] [Please call an ambulance.]

B 알겠습니다. 바로 도와드리겠습니다. Okay. I'll help you right away.

A 몸이 안 좋아요. I don't feel well.

B 어떻게 아프십니까? Where does it hurt?

A 언제부터 통증을 느끼셨어요? Since when have you been feeling pain?

[언제부터 통증이 시작되셨어요?] [When did the pain start?]

B 지난 밤부터요. Since last night.

A 약 복용하실 때 알레르기 같은 거 있으세요?
Do you have any allergies when you take medicine?

[약 복용하실 때 특이사항이 있으세요?]
[Are there any special precautions when taking the medication?]

[평소에 알레르기 반응이 나타나는 약이 있어요?]
[Do you have any medicine that gives you allergic reactions?]

B 네, 저는 땅콩 알레르기가 있어요. Yes, I'm allergic to peanuts.

[제 혈액형이 RH-예요.] [My blood type is RH negative.]

[저는 아스피린에 알레르기가 있어요.] [I'm allergic to aspirin.]

A 속이 쓰리는데, 약 좀 추천해 주시겠어요?
I have a stomach ache, can you recommend me some medicine?

B 이 약은 아주 순한 약이에요. 복용해 보세요.
This medicine is very mild. Try it.

A 열이 나고 목이 아파요. I have a fever and a sore throat.

B 우선 열을 재 봅시다. 해열제를 드릴게요.
Let's take your temperature first. I'll give you some fever reducer.

[우선, 체온을 좀 재겠습니다.] [First, let me take your temperature.]

[우선, 체온을 확인해 볼게요.] [First, let's check your temperature.]

A 며칠동안 설사를 하고 있어요. I've been having diarrhea for several days.

B 이 약을 드셔 보세요. 효과가 있을 거예요. Try this medicine. I think it will work.

A 약 때문인지 두통이 사라졌어요.
My headache went away, maybe because of the medicine.

B 다행입니다. 곧 좋아지시기를 바랍니다. What a relief! I hope you get better soon.

[다행이에요. 빨리 낫기 바랍니다. [What a relief. Hope you get better soon.]

A 이거 먹고 나면 나을까요? Will I be better after taking this?

B 너무 염려하지 마세요. 곧 괜찮아질 거예요. Don't worry too much. You'll be fine soon.

[너무 걱정하지 마세요. 곧 좋아질 거예요.]

[Don't worry too much. You'll get better soon.]

A 혈액형이 어떻게 됩니까? What is your blood type?

B 제 혈액형은 A형입니다. My blood type is A.

A 발목을 삐었어요. I sprained my ankle.

[열이 있어요.] [I have a fever.]

[상한 음식을 먹은 것 같아요.] [I think I ate something bad.]

B 엑스레이를 찍어야 됩니다. I need you to have an X-ray taken.

[주사를 놓겠습니다.] [I'll give you an injection.]

[이틀 동안 침대에 누워 계셔야 합니다.] [You need to stay in bed for two days.]

A 병원에 입원해야 하나요? Should I be admitted to the hospital?

B 일단 병원에 가서 의사를 만나보세요. First, go to the hospital and see a doctor.

5 Pronunciation 발음

Track 9-07

> ☑ 'ㅎ' Phonemic Omission('ㅎ' 약화)
>
> When ㅎ is followed by a ending or suffix in a vowel, the ㅎ sound is rarely pronounced.
>
> **Ex** 좋아요 → [조아요]   괜찮아요 → [괜차나요]   놓으세요 → [노으세요]   많아요 → [마나요]
> 싫어요 → [시러요]
>
> When the initial sound ㅎ follows a vowel, a nasal sound(ㅁ, ㄴ, ㅇ), or a liquid sound(ㄹ), the ㅎ sound is rarely pronounced.
>
> **Ex** 전화 → [저놔]   지하철 → [지아철]   실험 → [시럼]   영화 → [영와]
> 한국생활 → [한국생왈]

A

■ 다른 버스를 대절하도록 하겠습니다. We'll rent another bus.

⅃ 다른 버스를 부르도록 하겠습니다. We'll call another bus.

⅃ 다른 차량을 준비하도록 하겠습니다. We'll have another vehicle ready.

⅃ 다른 차를 호출하고 준비시키겠습니다. We'll call another car and get it ready.

A

■ 많이 놀라셨겠어요! You must have been very surprised!

⅃ 너무 놀라셨지요? You were surprised, right?

⅃ 무척 놀라셨을 것 같아요. I think you must have been very surprised.

A

■ 어디가 편찮으세요? Where does it hurt? (honorific)

⅃ 어디가 아프세요? Where does it hurt?

⅃ 어디가 불편하신가요? Where do you feel uncomfortable?

⅃ 어디가 안 좋으신 것 같으세요? Where does it seem to bother you?

A

■ 증상은 어떠세요? How are your symptoms?

⅃ 증세는 어떠세요? How are your symptoms?

⅃ 증세는 어떠신가요? How are your symptoms? (honorific)

⅃ 증상이 뭐예요? What are your symptoms?

⅃ 어떤 증세가 있으세요? What symptoms do you have?

7.1 Korea's Medical/Medicine Service System
한국의 의료&의약 서비스 체계

South Korea offers a universal healthcare system. After six months, foreigners living in South Korea must register for Korea's universal healthcare system. The healthcare system in South Korea is one of the best in the world for both foreigners and Koreans. Within just 12 years (1977–1989), South Korea was able to transition from a private healthcare system to government-mandated universal healthcare coverage. Currently, South Korea has a single-payer, publicly and privately financed program.

The biggest question among foreigners tends to be whether or not they should go to a hospital or clinic in South Korea. There are far more clinics than hospitals in Korea. 90% of physicians work in the private sector in Korea. However, most Koreans seek treatment at a hospital for the common cold. However, it is best to go to a hospital rather than a clinic if you have serious issues. For example, if you are looking for treatments for diabetic foot ulcers, do your research to find the best hospital for that particular issue. For both cases, after being examined by a doctor, you will be sent to a nearby pharmacy to pick up your prescription. All hospitals in Korea will have a pharmacy within the hospitals. In addition, most clinics in Korea will have a pharmacy within walking distance and sometimes within the same building.

In most cases, there is no need for private health insurance in South Korea. South Korea offers one of the best healthcare plans in the world. For those that are in good health and will only need to go to the hospital in emergencies, the NHI is the way to go. However, if you have health issues requiring constant treatment, it is highly recommended that you get private insurance since having only public insurance could be costly.

It is important to note that the quality of care between private and public healthcare is pretty much the same. Therefore, deciding between public vs. private depends on the time you will need to visit a hospital or clinic in Korea. In addition, plastic surgery in Korea is not covered under the national health insurance program. The cost of private health insurance in Korea is similar to public health insurance. It will typically range from 100,000 won to 120,000 won. However, if you get private health insurance, you are required to also pay for public health insurance.

7.2 10 Things to Do in Korean Daily Life for a Healthy Life
건강한 삶을 위한 일상 수칙 10가지

1) **Drinking 8 to 10 cups of water a day** : Coffee, juice, soda, and beer are counterproductive.

2) **Walking 50 minutes a day fast:** You need a habit of moving a lot.

3) **Generous and positive thinking to reduce stress** : find your own way of writing, crying, singing, etc.

4) **Basic habits of 'sufficient sleep' for immunity** : light and noise need to be blocked for six to eight hours of good sleep a day

5) **Eat whole vegetables and fruits to supplement vitamin C** : Maintain intestinal health with garlic and onions

6) **Drinking milk to replenish calcium** : minimal habits for bone health

7) **15 minutes of sun exposure for vitamin D synthesis:** Increase immunity and prevent various diseases and osteoporosis

8) **Supplement protein by eating meat and fish twice a week** : Maintain hip and thigh muscle strength through lower body exercises such as squats

9) **Having a doctor using a local clinic** : Understanding the status through vaccination and health examination and preventing diseases

10) **Eating breakfast 30 minutes after waking up** : Excellent for concentration, digestion, and weight control

7.3 The use of the Internet by Koreans 한국 사람들의 인터넷 활용

With the development of the Internet and information and communication technology, the method of transmitting news or exchanging information has also changed in various ways. Korea has a high Internet and smartphone penetration rate based on its advanced information and communication technology, and Koreans' daily lives are with the Internet.

The most common thing Koreans do on the Internet is searching for information. Koreans use online services by exchanging various information through the Internet in their daily lives all day long. The next most common tasks are reading news and newspapers, checking e-mail, shopping on the Internet and banking online.

The representative search portal sites used by Koreans are NAVER, Google, and Daum, which provide various services such as news, blogs, dictionaries, and maps as well as e-mail services. In particular, Koreans are using the function "Kakao Talk" of smartphones to exchange chatting, text messages, photos, and videos with many people anytime, anywhere.

As such, the Internet is closely connected to everyday life for Koreans, so even when traveling abroad, they want to choose a suitable mobile phone roaming method before departure and use the same Internet service as in Korea. Local tour guides are advised to share information on network services of carriers available at travel destinations or Wi-Fi-enabled areas with travelers.

🔖 Dialogue 1

(1) 손님들이 편히 쉬도록 조용히 했어요.

(2) 감기에 걸리지 않도록 손을 잘 씻어야겠네요

(3) 교환하지 않도록 옷을 입어보고 샀어요

(4) 밤새도록 이야기를 했어요

(1) 길이 막혔더라면 비행기를 놓칠 뻔했어요

(2) 아침에 늦게 일어났더라면 약속을 못 지킬 뻔했어요

(3) 신용카드가 없었더라면 지하철을 못 탈 뻔했어요

(4) 공부를 열심히 안 했더라면 대학교에 합격을 못 할 뻔했어요

🔖 Dialogue 2

(1) 식어 버렸어요. (2) 울어버렸어요. (3) 출발해 버렸어요. (4) 줘 버렸어요.

(1) 보고 싶을 때 (2) 먹을 때 (3) 나쁠 때 (4) 도착했을 때

(1) 일이 많아서 집에 못 가요.

(2) 길이 좁아서 차가 지나갈 수 없어요.

(3) 눈이 많이 내려서 비행기가 연착되었어요.

(4) 옷이 작아서 입기가 어려워요.

Answers

(1) 담배를 끊은 지 세 달이 지났어요.

(2) 휴대폰을 산 지 하루 만에 고장이 났어요.

(3) 한국어를 공부한 지 2년이 됐어요.

(4) 그 책을 읽은 지 오래돼서 내용이 잘 기억나지 않아요.

(1) 공연이 끝나고 나서 식당에 갈 거예요.

(2) 책을 다 읽고 나서 잠을 잤어요.

(3) 설거지를 하고 나서 빨래를 했어요.

(4) 친구가 가고 나서 갑자기 외로워졌어요.

(1) 편해져요.   (2) 끊어져요.   (3) 망설여져요.   (4) 기다려져요.

10

물병은 가방에 넣고 탑승하지 마세요
Don't put a bottle of water in your bag before boarding

Unit 10

물병은 가방에 넣고 탑승하지 마세요

Don't put a bottle of water in your bag before boarding

---

1 **Study Objectives** 학습 목표

✏ To guide airport use and introduce boarding etiquette
(공항 이용 안내와 탑승 에티켓)

✏ To use expressions related to responding to inquiries and solving requests for
help when using public institutions (공공기관 이용 시 문의와 도움 요청 해결)

✏ To provide guidance and support on the use of public facilities
(공공시설물 사용에 대한 안내와 지원)

---

2 **Vocabulary** 어휘

2.1 **Dialogue Vocabulary** 본문 어휘

Noun 명사 ✏

출국 departure	짐 luggage	물병 water bottle
탑승 boarding	액체류 liquids	수하물 baggage
밀리 리터 ml	호주 Australia	환율 exchange rate
미화 USD	교환 exchange	요청 request
소포 parcel	배편 by ship	항공편 by air flight

배송 shipping	비용 cost	무게 weight
파손 demage	보험 insurance	분실 loss

Verb 동사 🖊

섞다 mix up	부치다 send	바꾸다 change
환전하다 exchange money		

Others 나머지 🖊

보안 검색 security check	덕분에 thanks to	항공우편 airmail
국제우편 international mail	개인용품 personal goods	보험을 들다 buy an insurance
반입 금지물품 prohibited goods	수하물로 부치다 check in as baggage	
검색에 걸리다 be caught in a search		

2.2 Related Vocabulary 관련 어휘

은행 Bank 🖊

송금 remittance	안내 데스크 information desk	비밀번호 PIN
현금 cash	잔고 account balance	예금 bank deposit
현금 카드 ATM card	현금 인출기 ATM	서비스 요금 service charge
은행 창구 teller window	직불 카드 debit card	카드 소지자 card holder
입금액 deposit amount	부채 debt	이자 interest
대출 loan	공과금 utility bill	계좌 account
잔액 조회 balance check	계좌 이체 account transfer	
은행 거래기록 bank statement	계좌를 열다 open bank account	

우체국 Post Office ✏️

편지 letter	우표 stamp	주소 address
우체통 letterbox	물건 thing, stuff	저울 scale
요금 fare	발신인 sender	수신인 recipient
봉투 envelope	우편번호 zip code	집배원 mailman
창구 counter	포장 packaging	택배 parcel service
카운터 counter	등기우편 registered mail	국제 특급 EMS
날짜 date	퀵 서비스 quick service	포장하다 wrap up
붙이다 stick	반송하다 send back	깨지다 be broken
파손되다 be damaged	보관하다 store	답장을 보내다 send a reply
깨지기 쉬운 to be fragile	보통으로 보내다 send by regular mail	
속달로 보내다 send by express	등기로 보내다 send by registered mail	
소포를 보내다 send a package	우편번호를 쓰다 write zip code	

공항과 항공사 Airport and Airline ✏️

도착 arrival	환승 transfer	출발 departure
수하물 baggage	탑승구 flight gate	도착하다 arrive
짐꼬리표 baggage tag	탑승 boarding	활주로 runway
도심 터미널 city terminal	탑승수속 check-in	항공편 번호 flight No.
공동운항(좌석공유) codeshare	지연 delay	현지 시간 local Time
목적지 destination	출국신고서 embarkation card	안전벨트 safety belt
예약 초과 over booking	착륙하다 land	탑승권 boarding pass
대기 stand-by	전자 항공권 e-ticket	세관검사 customs inspection
탑승하다 board	이륙하다 take off	
수하물 찾는 곳 baggage claim	수하물 허용량 baggage allowance	
자동 출입국 automated immigration	세관을 통과하다 pass through custom	

머리 위 짐칸 overhead compartment

기내 반입 수하물 carry-on baggage

탑승수속 카운터 check-in counter

입국신고서 landing card

여객터미널 passenger terminal

위탁 수하물 checked baggage

연결편 비행기 connecting flight

대형 수하물 oversized baggage

공항 검색대를 통과하다 go through security

3 Dialogue 대화

| Dialogue 1 | **Departure gate 출국장** |

A 수고 많으셨어요. 그동안 가이드님 덕분에 즐거운 여행이었어요.
Thank you for your hard work. I had a great trip. Thanks to you.

B 감사합니다. 출국하시기 전에 다시 한번 짐을 확인해 주세요.
Thank you. Please check your luggage again before you leave the country.

항공기 내 반입금지물품은 알고 계시지요?

You know any prohibited items on the plane, don't you?

A 이 물병은 가져갈 수 있지요? Can I take this water bottlel?

B 보안검색에 걸릴 수 있습니다. You may get caught in a security scan.

물병은 가방에 넣고 탑승하지 마세요. Don't put the water bottle in your bag.

액체류 100 밀리리터 이상 물품은 반드시 수하물로 부치셔야 합니다.

Items over 100 ml of liquid must be checked in by baggage.

Key Grammar 핵심 문법

–지요?

1. It is used when the speaker wants to confirm with the listener.

–지요
모르다: 모르 + 지요 → 모르지요 알다: 알 + 지요 → 알지요

선생님 말씀대로 우리가 틀렸는지도 모르지요. We may be wrong, as you say.

제가 어떤 사람인지는 어머니가 더 잘 알지요. My mother knows better who I am.

어렸을 때 저는 운동을 꽤 잘했지요. I was pretty good at sports as a kid.

2. It is used when the speaker wants to obtain the listener's agreement about something already known.

어제는 무척 추웠지요? It was very cold yesterday, right?

오늘 날씨가 좋지요? Isn't the weather nice today?

세월이 참 빠르지요? Time flies, doesn't it?

☞ For present tense adjectives and verbs, '지요' is added to the stem. For past tense, adjectives and verbs, '–았/었지요' is added; for future tense verbs, '–(으)ㄹ 거지요' is added. In colloquial speech, '지요' is sometimes shortened to '죠'.

🍀 **Choose the appropriate word from the box and complete the following sentences using '지요' as in the example.**

> 예쁘다   있었다   맞다   오시겠다   마련이다

Ex 참, 어제 약속이 <u>있었지요</u>.

(1) 누구나 실수하기 _____.

(2) 늦어도 한 시까지는 _____?

(3) 여기가 시청 앞이 _____?

(4) 물론 안나 씨는 _____.

덕분에 ▶

It is used to express the reason for the positive result of an action or state. It corresponds to 'thanks to N' in English.

–덕분에
친구: 친구 + 덕분에 → 친구 덕분에 응원: 응원 + 덕분에 → 응원 덕분에

한국 친구 덕분에 내 한국어 실력은 날로 향상되고 있어요.

Thanks to my Korean friend, my Korean is improving day by day.

관중의 응원 덕분에 이번 경기에서 이겼어요.

Thanks to the support of the crowd, we won this game.

당신의 도움 덕분에 비행기를 놓치지 않았어요.

Thanks to your help, I didn't miss the flight.

☘ Fill in the blanks using the appropriate word in the box as in the example.

한국 친구	비타민	음악	장학금	가이드	날씨

Ex 선생님 덕분에 시험을 잘 봤어요.

(1) _____ 덕분에 좋은 대학을 다녔어요.

(2) 보내주신 _____ 덕분에 건강이 좋아졌어요.

(3) _____ 덕분에 한국 생활에 쉽게 적응할 수 있었어요.

(4) _____ 덕분에 여행이 편하고 즐거웠어요.

-지 마세요 ▼

It is an expression used to prohibit the act mentioned in the preceding statement politely. It corresponds to 'Don't do something' in English. It is attached to a verb stem, irrespective of whether the stem ends with a consonant or vowel.

–지 마세요
피우다: 피우 + 지 마세요 → 피우지 마세요 떠들다: 떠들 + 지 마세요 → 떠들지 마세요 찍다: 찍 + 지 마세요 → 찍지 마세요

여기서는 담배를 피우지 마세요. Don't smoke here.

도서관에서는 떠들지 마세요. Don't make a noise in the library.

미술관에서 사진을 찍지 마세요. Please don't take pictures in the art museum.

🍀 Fill in the blanks using the appropriate word in the box as in the example.

하다   내리다   먹다   보다   늦다   앉다

Ex 조형물에 <u>앉지 마세요</u>.

(1) 앞으로 수업 시간에 _____.

(2) 버스가 멈추기 전에는 _____.

(3) 버스 안에서는 음식을 _____.

(4) 수업 시간에는 휴대폰을 _____.

A 이걸 호주 달러로 환전하고 싶어요. I'd like to exchange this for Australian dollars.

여기서 환전이 되나요? Can I exchange money here?

B 네, 되고 말고요. 여권을 보여 주시겠어요?
Yes, of course. May I see your passport, please?

A 지금 환율이 어떻게 돼요? What's the exchange rate now?

B 오늘 환율로 1호주 달러가 77 US센트입니다.
At today's exchange rate, Australian dollar is 77 US cents.

A 그렇군요. 그럼 미화 300달러를 호주달러로 바꿔 주세요.
I see. Then, please change the US$300 to Australian dollars.

B 그러죠. 어떻게 교환해 드릴까요? Sure. How would you like it exchanged?

A 10달러와 20달러짜리를 섞어서 주실 수 있어요?
Can you mix 10 dollars and 20 dollars?

B 그럼요, 요청하신 대로 바꿔드리겠습니다. Certainly, I'll change it to your request.

-고 말고요

It is used to agree with the other person's question or the previous statement or emphasize that it really is or will do so. It roughly translates to 'of course', 'certainly' or 'it goes without saying'. It is attached to a verb stem or an adjective stem, irrespective of whether the stem ends with a consonant or vowel.

-고 말고요
복잡해지다: 복잡해지 +고 말고요 → 복잡해지고 말고요 먹다: 먹 + 고 말고요 → 먹고 말고요

제인 씨 부탁인데 가고말고요.

Because Jane asked a favor, I will definitely go.

신용카드를 쓰면 아주 편리하고말고요.

It goes without saying that using a credit card is very convenient.

외식하는 것이 집에서 요리하는 것 보다 더 비싸고 말고요.

Eating out is certainly more expensive than cooking at home.

🍀 **Complete the following sentences using '-고 말고요' as in the example.**

Ex   A: 내일 중요한 회의가 있는데 참석할 수 있어요?

B: <u>참석하고 말고요</u>. 몇 시까지 오면 돼요?

(1) A: 이 일이 내일까지 가능하지요?

B: _____. 내일 이 시간에 오십시오.

(2) A: 제주도가 그렇게 좋아요?

    B: _____. 가 보시면 아실 거예요.

(3) A: 서울의 대중교통이 시골보다 더 편하지요?

    B: _____. 교통카드 하나만 있으면 돼요.

(4) A: 한국에서 올 때 피곤했지요?

    B: _____. 비행기에서 계속 잤어요.

–는 대로

This expression is used with a verb to mean that it acts in the same way as in the preceding paragraph. It is attached to a verb stem, irrespective of whether the stem ends with a consonant or vowel.

–는 대로
하다: 하 + 는 대로 → 하는 대로
알다: 아 + 는 대로 → 아는 대로

제가 하는 대로 잘 따라 해 보세요. Please follow me as I do.

작품에 대해 아는 대로 설명해 주세요. Please explain the work as you know it.

생각 나는 대로 말해 주세요. Tell me what comes to your mind.

🍀 **Complete the following sentences as in the example.**

Ex 내가 <u>말하는 대로</u> 따라 하세요. (말하다)

(1) 날마다 _____ 만들었는데 오늘은 맛이 좀 이상해요. (만들다)

(2) 교통 사고에 대해 _____ 말해 주세요. (알다)

(3) 올해는 제가 _____ 다 되었으면 좋겠어요. (원하다)

(4) 예쁜 연예인인 "아이유'가 _____ 먹으면 다이어트에 성공할 거예요. (먹다)

A 무엇을 도와드릴까요? What can I do for you?

B 한국으로 소포를 보내려고 해요. I'm going to send a package to Korea.

A 배편으로 보내시겠어요? 항공편으로 보내시겠어요?
Would you like to send it by ship or air?

B 항공 우편으로 해 주세요. I'd like it by airmail, please.

A 포장을 제대로 하지 않으셨네요. You didn't wrap it properly.
죄송하지만 저쪽에서 다시 포장해 주세요.
I'm sorry, but please wrap it over there again.

B 여기 있습니다. Here it is.

지금 보내면 언제쯤 한국에 도착할까요? If I send it now, when will it arrive in Korea?

A 국제우편배송으로 7일 정도 걸릴 거예요.
It will take about 7 days by international mail delivery.

B 비용이 얼마나 드나요? How much does it cost?

A 무게 때문에 소포 비용이 달라집니다.
parcel costs vary due to weight.

이 소포에는 뭐가 들어 있나요? What's in this package?

B 개인용품이요. 의류하고 책이에요. It's for personal use. They are clothing and books.

A 이 물건에 우편보험을 드시겠어요? Would you like to have postal insurance on this?

B 파손보험은 들지 않고 분실보험만 들고 싶어요. I don't want damage insurance, but
loss insurance.

Key Grammar 핵심 문법

-지 않다

'-지 않다' is used to deny the act or state indicated in the preceding statement. It is short
for '-지 아니하다' and is attached to verbs and adjectives. 'V/A지 않다' expresses the same
notion as '안 V/A', which negates an action or a state. It is more formal than '안 V/A'. It is
simply attached to a verb stem or an adjective stem, irrespective of whether the stem ends
with a consonant or vowel.

-지 않다
마시다: 마시 + 지 않다 → 마시지 않다
춥다: 춥 + 지 않다 → 춥지 않다

저는 술을 마시지 않아요. I don't drink alcoholic beverage.

이 방이 좀 춥지 않아요? Isn't this room a bit cold?

이 가방은 무겁지 않아요. This bag is not heavy.

내일은 비가 오지 않을 거예요. It won't rain tomorrow.

🍀 **Use the expressions in parentheses to complete the following sentences as in the example.**

> Ex   <u>오늘은 학교에 가지 않아요.</u> (오늘은 학교에 가다)
>
>   <u>이 모자는 예쁘지 않아요.</u>   (이 모자는 예쁘다)

(1) _____. (어두운 곳에서 책을 읽다)

(2) _____. (저 모자는 비싸다)

(3) _____. (공항이 가깝다)

(4) _____. (저녁에 커피를 마시다)

-(으)려고 하다 ◢

It is attached to a verb stem to indicate the intention of an action or that it is an imminent movement. This pattern is a combination of the connective ending '-려고', indicating one's intent or situation, and the verb '하다'.

When the verb stem ends with a vowel and a consonant ㄹ → '-려고 하다'	When the verb stem ends with a consonant → '으려고 하다'
끝나다: 끝나 + 려고 하다 → 끝나려고 하다 만들다: 만들 + 려고 하다 → 만들려고 하다	찾다: 찾 + 으려고 하다 → 찾으려고 하다 앉다: 앉 + 으려고 하다 → 앉으려고 하다

회의가 벌써 끝나려고 해요. The meeting is about to end.

오늘 저녁에 불고기를 만들려고 해요. I'm going to fix bulgogi this evening.

은행에서 돈을 찾으려고 해요. I'm going to withdraw the money from the bank.

여기에 앉으려고 해요. I'm going to sit here.

♣ **Use the expressions in parentheses to complete the following sentences as in the example.**

> **Ex** 잡채를 만들려고 해요. (잡채를 만들다)

(1) _____. (배 표를 예매하다)

(2) _____. (한국 음식을 먹다)

(3) _____. (카페에서 책을 읽다)

(4) _____. (호텔에서 쉬다)

때문에

It expresses the reason for or cause of the situation described in the second clause and corresponds to 'because' in English. '때문에' is simply attached to a noun, irrespective of whether it ends with a consonant or vowel.

때문에
아기: 아기 + 때문에 → 아기 때문에
일: 일 + 때문에 → 일 때문에

아기 때문에 피곤해요. I'm tired because of the baby.

일 때문에 집에 갈 수 없어요. I can't go home because of work.

외국 여행을 할 때 음식 때문에 고생했어요.

I had a hard time with food when I traveled abroad.

🍀 **Use the words in parentheses to complete the following sentences as in the example.**

Ex 모기 때문에 잠자기 힘들어요. (모기 / 잠자기 힘들다)

(1) _____. (감기 / 목이 아프다)

(2) _____. (시험 / 늦게까지 공부했다)

(3) _____. (비 / 신발이 젖었다)

(4) _____. (눈 / 길이 미끄럽다)

4 **Response Exercise 응답 연습**

Getting airsick and feeling uncomfortable 비행기 멀미와 불편함 호소

Track 10-04

A 안색이 안 좋아 보이세요. 손님 괜찮으세요? You look pale. Are you OK?

B 속이 안 좋아요. 토할 것 같아요. I feel sick. I'm going to throw up.

A 그래요? 멀미용 봉지를 준비하겠습니다. Do you? Let me get the airsick bag ready.

B 비행기 멀미약 있어요? Do you have any pills for airsickness?

A 네, 곧 갖다 드리겠습니다. Yes, I'll bring it to you soon.

Complaints about airplane seats 비행기 좌석에 대한 불만

Track 10-05

A 통로 쪽 좌석으로 옮겨도 될까요? May I move to an aisle seat?

B 그럼요. 빈자리가 있다면요. Certainly, if there is a vacant seat.

A 좌석을 어떻게 눕히나요? How do I recline my seat?

B 팔걸이에 있는 버튼을 누르세요. Just push the button on your armrest.

A 도움이 필요하신가요? Do you need some help?

B 안전벨트가 걸려서 빠지지 않아요. he seatbelt got stuck and won't come off.

International call 국제 전화

Track 10-06

A 한국으로 국제전화를 부탁합니다. I'd like to make an international call to Korea.

B 네, 끊지 말고 기다려 주세요. 번호가 어떻게 되세요? Yes, please hold on. What's the number you want to call?

A 서울로 전화를 걸고 싶은데요? I'd like to make a call to Seoul, please?

B 국제 전화카드를 이용해 보세요. 1분에 40센트예요.
Try an international phone card. It's 40 cents a minute.

A 전화 카드를 어떻게 사용해요? How do I use a phone card?

B 카드 뒷면을 보시면 설명이 나와 있어요.
If you look at the back of the card, there is an explanation.

Post office 우체국

A 이 소포를 한국으로 보내고 싶어요. I'd like to send this package to Korea.

B 이 저울 위에 놓아 주세요. Please put it on this scale.

내용물이 무엇입니까? What are the contents?

A 물건을 어떻게 보내시겠어요? How would you like to send the item?

B 빠른 우편으로 보내고 싶어요. I'd like to send it by express mail.

A 포장용 상자를 파나요? Do you sell packing boxes?

B 네, 어떤 사이즈를 드릴까요? Yes, what size would you like?

[네, 어떤 사이즈를 원하세요?] [Yes, what size do you want?]

A 깨지기 쉬운 물건들은 버블랩을 사용해야 합니다. You should use bubble wrap for fragile items.

B 알겠습니다. 그럼 파손 조심 스티커도 붙여 주세요. All right. Then, please mark the box as fragile.

A 이 물건이 언제 도착할까요? When will this item arrive?

B 선박 우편으로 보내시면 3주 이상 걸립니다.

It will take more than three weeks if you send it by ship mail.

[항공편으로 보내실 경우 열흘쯤 걸릴 거예요.]

[It'll take about 10 days if you send it by air.]

[빠른 우편이니까 열흘 안에 갈 겁니다.]

[It's a fast mail, so it will be there in 10 days.]

Bank 은행

Track 10-08

A 오늘의 환율은 얼마인가요? What is today's exchange rate?

B 현재 환율은 뒤쪽 게시판에 있습니다.
The current exchange rate is on the bulletin board at the back.

A 환전을 하러 왔어요. I'm here to exchange money.

[달러를 밧으로 바꾸로 싶어요.] [I'd like to exchange dollar to baht.]

[달러를 밧으로 환전하고 싶어요.] [I want to exchange dollar to baht.]

B 번호표를 뽑고 잠시 기다려 주세요.
Please take your number ticket and wait a moment.

A 얼마를 환전해 드릴까요? How much would you like to exchange?

B 100 달러를 모두 밧으로 바꿔주세요. Please change all 100 dollars into baht.

A 이 수표를 현금으로 바꿀 수 있을까요? Can I cash this check?

B 네, 물론입니다. 어떻게 바꿔 드릴까요?
Yes, of course. How would you like to change it?

[네, 어떻게 교환해 드릴까요?] [Yes, how do you want it exchanged?]

[네, 어떻게 가져가시겠습니까?] [Yes, how do you want it exchanged?]

A 현금 자동 지급기는 어디에 있어요? Where is the ATM?

B 그 건물 1층 편의점 안에 있습니다.
It's in the convenience store on the first floor of the building.

5 Pronunciation 발음

 Pronunciation of '의' ('의' 발음)

Track 10-09

ᅴ is pronounced [ᅴ, ㅣ, ㅔ].

When ᅴ is used at the beginning of a word, ᅴ is pronounced [ᅴ].

Ex 의사 → [의사]   의자 → [의자]   의류 → [의류]   의미 → [의미]   의논 → [의논]
의견 → [의견]

When ᅴ is not the first syllable of a word, or when ᅴ is combined with an initial consonant other than 'ㅇ', ᅴ can be pronounced [ㅣ]

Ex 회의 → [회의/회이]   거의 → [거의/거이]   강의 → [강의/강이]   예의 → [예의/예이]
희망 → [희망/히망]

When ᅴ is used as possessive particle, ᅴ can be pronounced [ㅔ].

Ex 한국의 → [한국의/한국에]   친구의 → [친구의/친구에]   언니의→ [언니의/언니에]
우리의 → [우리의/우리에]

6 Additional Expression 추가 표현

A	◼ 이 소포에는 뭐가 들어 있나요? What's in this package?
	┘ 여기에는 어떤 물건이 담겨 있나요? What kind of stuff is in this?
	┘ 안에 들어있는 물건이 뭐예요? What's inside?

A	◼ 지금 환율이 어떻게 돼요? What's the exchange rate now?
	┘ 오늘 환율이 어떻게 되나요? What's the exchange rate today?
	┘ 지금 환율이 얼마인가요? What's the exchange rate now?
	┘ 원화 당 환율이 어떻게 되나요? What is the exchange rate per won?

B	1호주 달러가 77 US센트입니다. One Australian dollar is 77 US cents.
	[US달러당 호주달러 환율은 1.26입니다.]
	[The exchange rate for Australian dollars per US dollar is 1.26.]

A	▪ 어떻게 교환해 드릴까요? How would you like it exchanged?
	⌐ 어떻게 환전해 드릴까요? How would you like your money exchanged?
	⌐ 어떻게 바꿔 드릴까요? How would you like to change it?

A	▪ 가이드님 덕분에 즐거운 여행이었어요.
	Thanks to Mr._____ (Ms. _____), I(We) had a great trip.
B	그동안 함께 해 주셔서 감사합니다. Thank you for being with me till now.
	[그동안 감사했습니다. 안녕히 가세요.] [Thank you so much for everything, Good bye.]
	[감사합니다. 즐거운 여행 되셨기 바랍니다.] [Thank you. I hope you enjoyed your trip.]

7 Culture of Korea

7.1 National Airlines and Low Cost Carriers in Korea
한국의 국적항공사와 저비용 항공사

Aero_K

Aero K is a new low-cost airline based at Cheongju International Airport and has posted regular flights since April 2021. The interesting thing is that if you read the alphabet AeroK backwards, it becomes KoreA.

Air Premia

Air Premia is the first hybrid airline in Korea to operate Incheon International Airport as a hub, and it is a new concept airline that operates at a low-cost airline's good price with comfortable seats and premium services of large airlines.

Air Incheon

Air Incheon is Korea's only cargo-only airline and boasts a spectacular visual that does not appear to be a cargo plane. Although it was operating in the red, the amount of air freight transportation and freight rates increased due to COVID-19.

Hi Air

Hi Air is a small air carrier with limited seats, so even though it can accommodate up to 76 seats, it operates with 50 seats to enjoy the widest seat pitch among regular domestic seats.

FLY GANGWON

Fly Gangwon is a low-cost airline with Yangyang International Airport as its hub, and it has been temporarily closed since November 2020 due to low passengers and the influence of COVID-19, but now it is operating all routes again.

AIR SEOUL

Air Seoul is an airline launched by Asiana Airlines with 100% capital investment, and the name Air Seoul was built to mean that it is based on Incheon International Airport, the metropolitan area, in response to the existing Air Busan.

T'way

T'way Airlines, the first low-cost airline established in 2004, was discontinued due to financial difficulties, but after it was revived in 2010 and acquired by Yerimdang, it was changed to T'way Airlines and operates eight domestic and 55 international flights.

EASTAR JET

Eastar Jet is a South Korean low-cost airline that first launched in 2009 on the Gimpo-Jeju route. Although it was on the verge of bankruptcy due to worsening management, it is preparing to re-operate after being acquired by Sungjeong, a construction company.

AIR BUSAN

Air Busan is a low-cost airline established by local companies in Busan Metropolitan City, Busan, and Asiana Airlines, and is likely to change its parent company after the sale of Asiana Airlines, the largest shareholder, was decided.

JIN AIR

Jin Air is a low-cost airline founded by Korean Air with 100% investment and is supported by Korean Air's large infrastructure such as maintenance facilities, and even though it is a low-cost airline, it has medium and large aircraft and various types of aircraft.

JEJU air

Jeju Air is a private airline established in a joint venture between Jeju Special Self-Governing Province and Aekyung Group, and is the third-largest airline in Korea that launched international flights in 2009 for the first time as a low-cost airline in Korea.

ASIANA AIRLINES

Asiana Airlines announced that it was eventually decided to sell in 2019 and will be acquired and merged by Korean Air under the leadership of the Korea Development Bank as the debt rate continued due to financial difficulties of its parent company and the domestic airline industry.

KOREAN AIR

Korean Air is an airline affiliated with Hanjin Group, and is Korea's representative national airline that exclusively uses the English name "Korea" and Taegeuk design, which symbolizes Korea. It connects 125 cities in 44 countries.

7.2 International Airports in Korea 한국의 국제공항

Incheon International Airport 인천국제공항

An average of 1,097 aircraft enters and leaves the country daily, of which domestic flights account for 1% and international flights account for 99%. There are various international flights, including Europe, the United States, China, Southeast Asia, Australia, Russia, and Japan, and domestic flights are bound for Daegu and Gimhae. It is divided into Passenger Terminal 1 and Passenger Terminal 2. Passenger Terminal 2 is used by Korean Air and airlines belonging to "SKY TEAM," an airline association that includes KLM (Netherlands), Air France (France), and Delta Airlines (USA). All other airlines except those airlines use the Passenger Terminal 1.

Gimhae International Airport 김해국제공항

An average of 308 aircraft enters and leaves the country daily, of which domestic flights account for 40% and international flights 60%. There are international flights to China, Japan, Southeast Asia, and Australia, and domestic flights to Gimpo and Jeju. The peculiar thing is that Gimhae International Airport is a civilian and military airport. Therefore, military aircraft often enter and leave Gimhae International Airport, and workers from the Ministry of Land, Infrastructure and Transport and Air Force controllers are working together in the internal control facilities. And there is a flight time limit called Curfew at Gimhae International Airport. This limits the take-off and landing time of the aircraft due to noise problems near the airport, and the Gimhae International Airport Curfew is from 23:00 to 06:00 the next day, and the aircraft cannot take off or land at this time.

Jeju International Airport 제주국제공항

An average of 477 aircraft enters and leaves the country daily, of which 90% are domestic and 10% are international. International flights are bound for Southeast Asia, China, and Japan, and domestic flights have various routes such as Gimpo, Daegu, Gimhae, and Pohang. Recently, the proportion of aircraft entering and leaving China has been increasing. Jeju International Airport is often used by military aircraft because it is also used with the military.

Daegu International Airport 대구국제공항

An average of 87 aircraft enters and leaves the country daily, of which domestic flights account for 40% and international flights account for 60%. International flights are bound for Japan, Southeast Asia, and China, and domestic flights are bound for Gimpo, Jeju, and Incheon. And Daeguk International Airport is also a civilian−military public airport, so military aircraft enter and exit, and this airport is based on a large air base called the 11th Fighter Wing, so it is used by quite a lot of military aircraft compared to other international airports. Curfew is also present at this airport, and the hours are from midnight (00:00) to 05:00.

Cheongju International Airport 청주국제공항

An average of 48 aircraft enters and leaves the country daily, of which 80% are domestic and 20% are international. International flights are bound for Southeast Asia and China, and domestic flights are bound for Jeju. Most of these airports are Jeju's inbound and outbound routes, and there are occasional irregular international flights to Southeast Asia and China. And this airport is often used by aircraft for training.

Muan International Airport 무안국제공항

An average of 19 aircraft enters and departs a day, of which 20% are domestic and 80% are international. International flights are bound for Southeast Asia and domestic flights are bound for Jeju. For an international airport, there are few international flights using this airport and irregular international flights to Southeast Asia are available.

Yangyang International Airport 양양국제공항

An average of one aircraft enters and leaves the port every day. International flights are bound for Southeast Asia, and domestic flights are bound for Jeju, which is also an irregular flight. Recently, an airline called Fly Gangwon has been created, and the number of Jeju—Yangyang routes is increasing.

Answers — Dialogue 1

(1) 마련이지요.   (2) 오시겠지요.   (3) 맞지요.   (4) 예쁘지요.

(1) 장학금   (2) 비타민   (3) 한국 친구   (4) 날씨

(1) 늦지 마세요.   (2) 뛰지 마세요.   (3) 먹지 마세요.   (4) 보지 마세요.

Answers — Dialogue 2

(1) 가능하고 말고요.   (2) 좋고 말고요.   (3) 편하고 말고요.   (4) 피곤하고 말고요.

(1) 만드는 대로   (2) 아는 대로   (3) 원하는 대로   (4) 먹는 대로

Answers — Dialogue 3

(1) 어두운 곳에서 책을 읽지 않아요.   (2) 저 모자는 비싸지 않아요.

(3) 공항이 가깝지 않아요.   (4) 저녁에 커피를 마시지 않아요.

(1) 배 표를 예매하려고 해요.   (2) 한국 음식을 먹으려고 해요.

(3) 카페에서 책을 읽으려고 해요.   (4) 호텔에서 쉬려고 해요.

(1) 감기 때문에 목이 아파요.   (2) 시험 때문에 늦게까지 공부했어요.

(3) 비 때문에 신발이 젖었어요.   (4) 눈 때문에 길이 미끄러워요.

🍀 Depending on the purpose of the greeting 인사 목적에 따라

1	만남과 헤어짐

1.1	Daily encounter 일상 만남

A	일상 Daily	◼ 안녕하세요? 안녕하십니까? 안녕
		◼ 요즘 어떻게 지내세요? 잘 지내지? 별일 없지?
		◼ 안녕하세요? 어디 가세요? 안녕, 어디 가?
	아침 Morning/Breakfast	◼ 안녕히 주무셨어요? 편히 주무셨어요? 잘 잤어요? 잘 잤니? 아침 식사하셨어요?

점심 Lunch	■ 점심 식사하셨어요? 점심 드셨어요? 식사했어요? 밥 먹었어요? 밥 먹었니?	
저녁 Dinner/Evening	■ 저녁 드셨어요? 저녁 식사 맛있게 하세요.	
밤 Night	안녕히 주무세요. / 편히 주무세요.	
N 전/후 Before/After 주말/휴가/연휴/방학 Weekend/Vacation/ Holiday/School Break	■ 주말 잘 보내세요. 주말 잘 보내십시오. 주말 잘 지내. ■ 좋은 시간 보내세요.	

1.2 First meeting 처음 만남

A	■ 안녕하세요? 처음 뵙겠습니다. (저는 ooo라고 합니다/ 저는 ooo입니다.) 만나서 반갑습니다. (저는 ooo라고 합니다/ 저는 ooo입니다.) 반갑습니다. 말씀 많이 들었습니다. 잘 부탁드립니다. (저는 ooo입니다.) 뵙게 되어 반갑습니다.
B	안녕하세요. 반갑습니다. 안녕하세요. 저도 만나서 반갑습니다. ooo입니다. 반갑습니다. 처음 뵙겠습니다. ooo입니다. 네, 안녕하세요. 저도 말씀 많이 들었습니다. 반갑습니다. 저는 ooo입니다. 저도 잘 부탁드립니다.

1.3 **Long time no see** 오랜만의 만남

A1	🔲 오랜만이에요. (그동안) 잘 지냈어(요)? / 잘 지내셨어요? 오랜만이야. (오래간만이야). 그동안 잘 지냈지? (그동안) 어떻게 지냈어(요)? 잘 지내고 있지(요)?
A2	🔲 오래간만입니다. 그동안 안녕하셨어요? 요즘 어떻게 지내셨어요? 오랜만에 뵙네요. 요즘 어떻게 지내요?
A3	🔲 안녕하세요? 오랜만이에요. 반가워. 얼마만이지? 아니, 이게 누구야? 정말 반갑다.
B	안녕하세요? 정말 오래간만이에요. 안녕하세요? 저도 덕분에 잘 지내고 있어요. 반가워요. 잘 지내고 있어요. 그동안 잘 지냈어? 나도 반갑다.

1.4 **Daily farewell** 일상 헤어짐

A1	🔲 안녕히 가세요. 안녕히 가세요. 다음에(나중에) (또/다시) 뵙겠습니다. 조심히(조심해서) 들어가세요. 살펴가세요. 잘 가요. 안녕, 잘 가

A2	☐ 다음에 만나요. 내일 만나요. / 내일 뵙겠습니다/ 이따 뵐게요. 이따 봐(요). 다음에 보자. / 다음에 봐(요). / 내일 보자. / 연락하자. 언제 다시 만날 수 있어요?
A3	☐ 나중에(다음에) 뵙겠습니다. (ㅇㅇ에게도) 안부 좀 전해주세요. 나중에(다음에) 연락할게(요). 전화할게요.
A4	☐ 언제 밥 한번 먹어요. 언제 식사나 한번 같이 해요. 다음에 같이 밥 먹자. 언제 한번 술 한 잔 하자.
A5 **모임** **회식** Get-together dinner	☐ 죄송해요. 저 먼저 갈게요. 일이 있어서 먼저 가 봐야 할 것 같아요. 먼저 실례하겠습니다. 다음에 다시 뵐게요. 죄송합니다. 일이 있어서 먼저 일어나겠습니다. 먼저 갈게. 오늘 즐거웠어.
B	안녕히 계세요. 안녕히 계십시오. 네, 다음에 (다시) 만나요. (봐요.) 오늘 만나서 즐거웠어요. 만나서 반가웠어요. 또 봐요.

1.5 **Long seperation** 오랫동안의 헤어짐

A	☐ 잘 다녀오세요. / 잘 다녀와. 몸조심해서 잘 다녀오세요. 너무 섭섭하네요. 몸 건강히 잘 다녀오세요. 잘 다녀오세요. 다시 봬요.

B	다녀오겠습니다.
	다녀와서 다시 뵙겠습니다.
	당분간 못 뵙겠네요. 잘 계세요.
	연락 드릴게요. 건강하시기 바랍니다.
	다음에 만나요.

2   Thank 감사

A1	■ 고맙습니다. / 감사합니다.
	고마워(요). / 감사해(요).
	그 동안 고마웠어.
	고맙다.
A2	■ 아/어/여서 고맙습니다. / 감사합니다.
	Ex) 시간 내 주셔서 고맙습니다.
	아/어/여 줘서 (정말) 고마워요. / 감사해요.
	Ex) 도와줘서 고마워요.
A3	■ 아/어/여서 감사합니다.
	~해 줘서 (정말) 감사합니다.
B	뭘요. (아닙니다. / 아니예요).
	별 말씀요.
	고맙기는(요).
	고맙기는요. 별것도 아닌데요.

A1	■ 축하합니다. / 축하드립니다. 축하드려요. 축하해요. 정말 잘 됐어요. 축하한다. 축하해.
B	감사합니다. 고맙습니다. 고마워(요). 감사해(요).

A1	■ 잘 하네요. 잘 하시네요. Ex 한국말을 참 잘하시네요.
A2	■ 대단하세요. 와, 대단하십니다. 정말 대단하시네요.
A3	■ 훌륭하십니다. / 훌륭합니다. 좋습니다. 훌륭하네요.
A4	■ 좋아요. 좋네요.
B	감사합니다. 고맙습니다. 별 말씀을요. 아니에요. 별 말씀을요. 칭찬 감사합니다. 아직 많이 부족해요.

A1	■ 미안합니다. / 죄송합니다.
	정말 미안해(요). / 죄송해요.
	오히려 제가 미안한데요.
	미안해서 어떻게 하죠? / 미안해서 어쩌죠?
	미안해. 내가 잘못했어.
A2	■ -아/어/여서 미안합니다. / 죄송합니다.
	Ex 늦어서 미안합니다.
	-아/어/여서 미안해요. / 죄송해요.
	Ex 기다리게 해서 죄송해요.
A3	■ (제가) 잘못했어요. 죄송해요.
	실수를 했군요. 죄송합니다.
	제 실수예요. 미안해요.
A4	■ 제 잘못입니다. 주의하도록 하겠습니다.
	죄송합니다. 사과드립니다.
	죄송합니다. 앞으로 이런 일이 없도록 하겠습니다.
A5	■ 잘못했어요. 용서해 주세요.
	미안해, 용서해 줘.
	미안하다. 용서해라.
B	미안하기는(요), 괜찮아요.
	(아니), 괜찮아요.
	미안하기는요. 별 일도 아닌데요.
	아니에요.
	오히려 제가 미안해요.

5	**Request 부탁, 요청**

A1	■ 실례합니다. / 실례하겠습니다. 저, 실례합니다.
A2	■ 저기요, 실례지만 / 실례합니다만 저기요, 죄송하지만 / 죄송합니다만
A3	■ 부탁이 있는데요. 부탁드릴 게 있는데(요) 부탁이 있는데 좀 들어줄 수 있어(요)?
A4	■ (내가) 부탁이 있는데 내가 부탁할 게 좀 있는데, 얘기해도 될까(요)?
B	네, (말씀하세요.) 뭔데요? 말씀하세요. 네, 그래요. 무슨 부탁인데(요)?

6	**Rejection 거절, 사양**

B	죄송합니다. / 미안합니다. (아닙니다.) 괜찮습니다. 사양하겠습니다. (사양할게요.) 미안하지만 어렵겠습니다. 죄송합니다. 죄송한데, 그건 좀 곤란합니다. 나도(저도) 그러고 싶지만 안 되겠어요. 죄송해요. 좀 부담스럽네요. 생각을 해 보겠습니다. 다른 사람(분)에게 부탁해 보세요. 죄송합니다. (저에게) 이런 부탁 하지 마세요. 아니요. 아닙니다. 싫은데요.

A1	■ 걱정하지 마세요. 너무 걱정하지 마(세요). 걱정 마.
A2	■ 잘 될 거예요. 잘 할 수 있을 거예요. 곧 좋아질 거예요.
A3	■ 괜찮아요. 괜찮을 거예요. 곧 괜찮아질 거예요. 괜찮아.
A4	■ 많이 힘들지요? 힘 내세요.
B	감사합니다. / 고맙습니다. 네, 고마워요. 그렇게 되면 좋겠어요. 고마워요. ○○ 씨.

 Depending on situation 상황에 따라

새해 New year	새해 복 많이 받으세요. 한 해 동안 고생 많으셨습니다. 새해 복 많이 받으세요. 새해에 원하시는 일 모두 이루시기 바랍니다. 올 한 해도 건강하시고 좋은 일 가득하시기 바랍니다.
명절 National holiday	즐거운 명절 보내세요. 명절과 연휴, 잘 보내세요. 친지들과(가족들과) 좋은 시간 보내세요. 설(추석) 지나고 뵙겠습니다. 좋은 시간 보내세요.

결혼식 Wedding Ceremony	축하드려요. 축하드립니다. 두 분 너무 잘 어울려요. 결혼 축하드려요. 오래오래 행복하시고 잘 사시기 바랍니다. 신랑, 신부 모두 너무 예쁘고 멋지세요. 축하드려요.
집들이 Housewarming	어서 오세요. 환영합니다. 어서 오세요. 바쁘실텐데 와 주셔서 감사합니다. 뭘 이런 걸 사 오세요, 그냥 오시지. 감사합니다. 차린 건 없지만 많이 드세요. 음식이 입에 맞을지 모르겠네요. 맛은 없지만 많이 드세요.
생일 Birthday	생일 축하해요. 생신 축하드립니다. 행복하고 즐거운 하루 보내세요. 건강하게 오래오래 사세요.
돌잔치 First birthday party	축하드립니다. 축하드려요. 좋으시겠어요. 아기가 너무 예뻐요. 귀여워요. 아기가 엄마를 닮아서 예쁘네요. 아기가 예뻐서 좋으시겠어요. 아기도 예쁘고 엄마, 아빠 모두 너무 멋지세요. 돌잔치 준비하느라 힘드셨죠? 여기 분위기도 좋고 음식도 맛있네요. 아기 예쁘게 잘 키우세요. 아기가 건강하게 잘 자라기 바랍니다.
조문 Condolences	고인의 명복을 빕니다. 삼가 조의를 표합니다. 얼마나 상심이 크시겠어요. (아무 말도 하지 않는다) 상심이 크시겠어요. 뭐라고 위로의 말씀을 드려야 할지…..(아무 말도 하지 않는다) 많이 슬프시겠어요. 고인의 명복을 빕니다.
병문안 Visit to a sick person	빨리 회복하시기 바랍니다. 빨리 나으시기 바랍니다. 많이 안 다쳐서 다행이에요(다행이다) 괜찮아요? 많이 걱정했어(요). 빨리 낫기를 바라(요).

서비스 한국어

초판발행   2025년 2월 28일

지은이   김은영·김공환
펴낸이   안종만·안상준

편 집   조영은
기획/마케팅   박부하
표지디자인   이은지
제 작   고철민·김원표

펴낸곳   ㈜ 박영사
              서울특별시 금천구 가산디지털2로 53, 210호(가산동, 한라시그마밸리)
              등록 1959.3.11. 제300-1959-1호(倫)

전 화   02)733-6771
f a x   02)736-4818
e-mail   pys@pybook.co.kr
homepage   www.pybook.co.kr
ISBN   979-11-303-2141-7   03710

copyright©김은영·김공환, 2025, Printed in Korea

* 파본은 구입하신 곳에서 교환해드립니다. 본서의 무단복제행위를 금합니다.

정 가   27,000원